Contents

Preface

I have followed the rise and development of liberation theology from the very beginning. In summer 1971 I read the typescript of *Teología de la liberación* by Gustavo Gutiérrez, the book with which this new theological approach began, published in its first Peruvian edition in Lima in December 1971 and in an Italian edition in March 1972 (American and English editions followed in 1973 and 1974 respectively). From then on I have followed the main stages of a theological process which has proved to be increasingly lively and enthralling. In particular I would like to recall my meetings with the main liberation theologians which are recorded, together with a survey of this new factor in theology and the church, in a book which I edited entitled *New Frontiers of Theology in Latin America* (1975), published in English by Orbis Books and SCM Press in 1980; my involvement in the great theological congress on 'Liberation and Captivity' held in Mexico City from 11 to 15 August 1975 on the occasion of the fifth centenary of the birth of Fra' Bartolomé de las Casas, followed immediately by the 'Theology in the Americas' conference held in Detroit between 17 and 23 August which represented the first real encounter between Latin American liberation theology, black theology and feminist theology, and which led people for the first time to talk of 'theologies of liberation' in the plural; and my involvement in the international ecumenical congress promoted by EATWOT (the Ecumenical Association of Third World Theologians) in São Paolo, Brazil, from 20 February to 2 March 1980 on the theme of liberation theology. So I have had the opportunity on many occasions in a professional context to meet theologians and pastors as well as to follow through the literature showing the development of a theological reflection which has come to take on increasingly wide dimensions, and which certainly represents one of the most colourful and creative, as well as one of the most controversial, chapters in the theology of our century. The two recent Vatican documents – the *Instruction on Certain Aspects of the Theology of Liberation* of August 1984 and the *Instruction on Christian Freedom and Liberation* of March 1986 – have led to international interest and debate going far beyond the boundaries of the church.

This book has arisen out of lecture series and conferences and earlier writings;[1] it sets out to present a general account of liberation theology, investigating its origins, examining its method, analysing the problems associated with it, reconstructing and summing up the controversies, outlining developments and prospects, and putting liberation theology in the wider context of Third World theology and the current theological debate.

The appendix contains two theological interviews, the first with Gustavo Gutiérrez, who surveys the course of his theological career; the second with Clodovis Boff, who discusses the difficulties faced by liberation theology.

Brescia, 23 August 1986

1 · The Origin and Method of Liberation Theology

According to the historical reconstruction proposed by Enrique Dussel,[1] Latin American liberation theology has its roots in the line of prophetic theology of the Latin American church which found expression in the non-academic theology of brave missionaries at the time of the Conquest – from 1511, the year in which the first critical and prophetic cry in Latin America was recorded, uttered by Antonio de Montesinos (died 1545) on behalf of the *indios* against the colonialist exploiters. Among the first generation of these missionary theologians Bartolomé de las Casas, José de Acosta and Bernardino de Sahagún should be especially remembered. This is a prophetic line which blossomed again in many periods through other figures and in other historical situations, in particular in the practical political theology at the time of neo-colonial emancipation at the beginning of the last century (Hidalgo and Morelos), and it is making a vigorous reappearance in the second half of this century with the theology of liberation.

A theology from the underside of history

Liberation theology is a complex phenomenon in which we can already identify several stages.

1. The *preparatory* phase (1962-1968): from the beginning of Vatican II with its programme of *aggiornamento* to the second conference of the Latin American episcopate at Medellín, which marked the acceptance of the Council by the Latin American church.

2. The *formative* phase (1968-1975): from the 1968 Medellín conference to 1975, the year in which the main theological studies from the new perspective had already become available and in which at the Detroit 'Theology in the Americas' conference (August 1975) the Latin American liberation theologians made their first contacts with the other forms of liberation theology, like black theology and feminist theology, and began to speak of 'liberation theologies' in the plural.

It is possible to sub-divide this second phase further, into: (*a*) the period of formulation in the strict sense (1968-1972): from the Medellín conference to 1972, the year in which liberation theology lost its initial euphoria and 'discovered the political time of captivity, prudence and patience';[2] and (*b*) a subsequent period characterized by its adoption of the theme of 'captivity and exile' (from 1972), which found articulate expression above all in Leonardo Boff's *Theology of Captivity and Liberation* (1975): 'There is no longer the euphoria of the 1960s, when it was possible to dream of popular liberation on a spectacular scale'.[3] Rubem Alves also wrote in his autobiographical article 'From Paradise to the Desert' (1975): 'The exodus of which we dreamed earlier has miscarried. Instead we now find ourselves in a situation of exile and captivity.'[4]

3. The *systematizing* phase (from 1976) when, with the theologians of the new generation, a period begins which sees liberation theology involved in reflecting on its methods and in systematic rethinking of the main themes of theology, especially christology and ecclesiology, in the new perspective. Moreover this is when, with the formation of the Ecumenical Association of Third World Theologians (1976), liberation theology found a place in the broader context of Third World theology.

The first outline of liberation theology was presented by Gustavo Gutiérrez at a conference held in the city of Chimbote, Peru, in July 1968, several weeks before the Medellín conference (24 August to 6 September 1968) and published the following year under the title 'Towards a Theology of Liberation' (1969);[5]

2

successive development and deepening of this approach resulted in his *Theology of Liberation*, which appeared in Lima in December 1971 and was the first systematic discussion.[6] However, Gutiérrez's book was simply the tip of an iceberg; liberation theology rapidly marked itself out as a new frontier of theology and as a movement in the church. In May of the same year there appeared Hugo Assmann's book *Opresión – Liberación. Desafío a los cristianos*, which was taken up and developed in *Theology for a Nomad Church* (1973);[7] July 1972 saw the publication of *Jesus Christ Liberator* by the Brazilian theologian Leonardo Boff.[8] These are the first texts which gave expression to the new theological course.[9]

Liberation theology came into being before the Medellín conference and inspired some of its documents, in particular the first one on Justice and the second on Peace;[10] and Medellín in turn, though never using the technical expression 'liberation theology', did make wide use of the category of 'liberation', and thus influenced the process which led to the development of the new theological project on a continental scale: 'We can claim that the idea of liberation and the theology of liberation acquired ecclesial status at the Medellín conference'.[11] Hence it proved possible to write that liberation theology is 'the spirit of Medellín distilled into a theology' (E.Schillebeeckx).[12] The Medellín conference, which had on its agenda the theme 'The Church in the Present Transformation of Latin America in the Light of the Council', did not just result in an application of the statements of the Council to the situation in Latin America but also set in motion a 'creative review of the Council from the perspective of the poor'.[13]

Notwithstanding the long and laborious preparations for it, the third conference of the Latin American episcopate at Puebla (27 January to 13 February 1969), on the theme 'The Evangelization of Latin America in the Present and in the Future',[14] resulted in 'a serene affirmation of Medellín'.[15] There is a bold and committed statement in the closing document: 'We affirm the need for conversion on the part of the whole church to a preferential

3

option for the poor, an option aimed at their integral liberation' (no.1134). The term 'integral', which often goes with the term liberation in the Puebla document, 'is meant to stress that this liberation cannot forget either the interior and personal aspect (liberation from personal sin) or the historical aspect (liberation from the current economic, social, political and cultural situation described as social sin)'. That notwithstanding, in essence it could be said that the Puebla texts focus attention mainly on this second aspect.[16]

The theology of liberation arose out 'of an ethical indignation at the poverty and marginalization of the great masses of our continent' (L.Boff); it is a theology lived out and written 'from the underside of history' (G.Gutiérrez). Hugo Assmann's justification for it is typical: 'If the historical situation of dependence and domination of two-thirds of humanity, with its thirty million deaths per year from hunger and malnutrition, does not now become the starting point for any Christian theology, in the rich and dominant countries as well, theology will no longer be able to locate and give specific historical expression to its basic themes... For this reason "it is necessary to save the church from its cynicism".'[17]

The theology of liberation is not just one more 'theology of...': it does not so much put forward a new theme (as for instance does the theology of secularization), as a new way of doing theology. To avoid the theology of liberation being conceptually mistaken for a 'theology of...', H.Assmann also avoids the grammar of the expression 'theology of liberation' and speaks of *'teologia desde la praxis de la liberación* (= theology starting from the praxis of liberation)'; others speak of 'theological reflection in a context of liberation'. Whereas in *La pastoral de la Iglesia en América Latina* (1968) – a text which is still beyond the new theological threshold – Gutiérrez defined theology as 'a critical function of the pastoral action of the church',[18] in *Theology of Liberation* he defines it as 'critical reflection from historical praxis in the light of faith'.[19] This definition is later made even more precise in an essay in *The Power of the Poor in History*: 'Theology in this context will be a critical reflection both from within, and upon, historical praxis, in confrontation with the word of the Lord as lived and experienced in faith.'[20]

Here theology is rigorously understood as a second act which presupposes a first act, on which it reflects. An authentic Christian theology is always a second act which presupposes a first act on which to reflect: according to Anselm's classic formulation it is *fides quaerens intellectum*; theological understanding presupposes faith, an experience of faith, in other words a spirituality, as its first act: 'All it does is make us aware that a theology that is not located in the context of an experience of faith is in danger of turning into a kind of religious metaphysics or a wheel that turns in the air without making the cart advance.'[21] So experience of faith is a first act; theology comes afterwards: theology as a second act. But the theology of liberation: (*a*) rigorously understands itself as a second act; (*b*) the first act presupposed is an experience of faith contextualized by commitment for the other (contextualized theology); is militant in the struggle for liberation (militant theology); is a praxis (a more adequate term than practice, experience, action, life, all of which could have an exclusively spiritual and personal connotation), indeed is a 'totality of practices', aimed at changing reality, at transforming relationships of dependence and domination. It is a 'theology of the faith which acts'; it is a theology *from* and *on*, which begins *from* praxis and reflects *on* the praxis of committed Christian communities; it is a reflection which accompanies communal paths of liberation: just as there are popular movements of liberation, so too there is also a theology of liberation. Here faith does not suddenly become discourse on history, but praxis in history, on which theology is called to reflect. According to Leonardo Boff's definition it has a christological connotation: 'The theology of liberation therefore means critical reflection on human praxis (of human beings generally and Christians in particular) in the light of the praxis of Jesus and the demands of the faith.'[22]

The key word 'liberation' is the correlative of 'dependence'

5

and made its first appearance in the new historical context in the 1960s in the context of sociology and pedagogics. As early as 1961 the French writer from Martinique, Frantz Fanon, had published in Paris a violent indictment of colonialism under a title which became famous, *The Wretched of the Earth*. It had a harsh preface by Jean-Paul Sartre, which among other things affirmed: 'The Third World finds *itself* and speaks to *itself* through this voice.' And again: '...Europe is springing leaks everywhere. What then has happened? It simply is that in the past we made history and now it is being made of us. The ratio of forces has been inverted, decolonization has begun; all that our hired soldiers can do is to delay its completion.'[23] The years between the Bandung Conference of 1955 and the Algiers Conference of 1973 mark the end of the colonial era.

A change took place after 1964, an 'epistemological rupture' in the sphere of the social sciences in Latin America: on the basis of new observations and analyses of the underdeveloped world put forward by Raul Prebish, the theory of dependence was developed (André Gunder Frank, Theotonio dos Santos, Celso Furtado, Fernando Henrique Cardoso) as a critique of the theory of development (*desarrolismo*). Latin America is not in a retarded state of underdevelopment, so that an organic system of aid from developed countries could help it to evolve towards the stage of development, indeed into a state of structural equilibrium: the underdevelopment is the by-product of the development of the developed countries. The underdeveloped peoples are in a state of 'dependence' – and not in a relationship of interdependence – which cannot be overcome with a linear and gradual process of development.[24] 'Liberation... expresses the inescapable element of radical change which is foreign to the ordinary use of the term development.'[25]

As the concept of 'development' – understood not only as economic growth but as a global social process in a humanistic perspective – had been introduced from the social sciences into the documents of the *magisterium* (*Mater et magistra*, 1961; *Pacem in terris*, 1963; *Gaudium et spes*, 1965; and above all

6 Essays in Black Theo, Univ. of Christian Movement, Johann- esburg 1922

Populorum progressio, 1967) and theological reflection, shaping a 'theology of development' (J.Alfaro, J.-M.Aubert, J.-Y.Calvez, F.Houtart, R.Laurentin),[26] so now the concept of 'liberation' entered into Latin American church documents and became the underlying category for a new theological programme: 'In the present Latin-American historical context... the theological and political theme of "liberation" is the evident "correlate" of the socio-political theme of "dependence". This latter marks the beginning of a new line in Latin American social sciences...; by analogy, the political theological theme of "liberation" opens up a new context and a new methodology of Christian reflection on faith as praxis with a precise situation in history.'[27]

It does not follow from this that the theology of liberation is indissolubly bound up with the sociological theory of dependence; this theory is only one of the interpretative instruments of social reality in Latin America, and has been taken up critically by liberation theology and integrated with other analyses which identify other causes (like the existence of oligarchical structures within the same Latin American reality).[28] To explain the complex social reality of Latin America it is not enough to limit oneself to a single monocausal explanation; rather, reference must be made to a 'whole web of causes and historical constellations'[29] which the social sciences investigate, thus bringing integration or correction to the theory of dependence.

The awareness of underdevelopment as an effect of the bad organization of the world had meanwhile kept on spreading. With the UNO declaration of 1 May 1974, signed by the Third World countries, the world community was presented with a collective plan for setting up a new international economic order.[30]

The concept of 'liberation' appeared not only in the sphere of the social sciences but also in the pedagogical field, in the works of the Brazilian pedagogue Paulo Freire, *Education as the Practice of Freedom* (1967)[31] and *The Pedagogy of the Oppressed* (1971).[32] He put forward the methodological approach – tested in praxis among movements of popular culture – of a 'liberating education',

7

an education, that is, not only aimed at literacy but understood as the practice of freedom, as an act of consciousness which offers help towards a critical reading of reality, as a process of conscientization: 'It was a typical attempt to get away from underdevelopment by means of a cultural operation.'[33]

The introduction of the language of 'liberation' into theology represents a significant linguistic innovation in that it brings about a shift of the semantic axis of the word 'freedom' and a recovery of the historical and dynamic force of biblical language. In its theological usage the concept of liberation has three levels:[34] (a) the socio-political level, i.e. liberation of the oppressed: 'exploited classes, despised ethnic groups, and marginalized cultures';[35] (b) the anthropological level: liberation for a qualitatively different society with a human dimension; (c) the theological level: liberation from sin, the ultimate root of all injustice and oppression, for a life of community and participation. And it is the task of a responsible theology of liberation to go through these three levels and articulate them in a differentiated account.[36]

Theology and praxis

From the beginning, the theology of liberation has understood itself as a new way of doing theology, but it has indicated its epistemological foundations in a somewhat intuitive and fragmentary way. Clodovis Boff has discussed the methods of liberation theology (and more generally of theological reflection which has the political sphere as its theme) in a thorough study on the relationships between *Theology and Praxis* (1978).[37] Using the epistemological analysis made by C.Boff, Leonardo Boff describes the theology of liberation in a fuller way: 'The theology of liberation tries to articulate a reading of reality beginning from the poor and with a concern for the liberation of the poor; to do this it uses the humane sciences and the social sciences, engages in theological meditation and calls for pastoral actions which help the way of the oppressed.'[38] This passage brings out very clearly the four elements which structure discussion in the theology of liberation: first an option and then three mediations. By mediation is meant the complex of means (the instruments) which theology uses to achieve its goal.

1. First of all the theology of liberation presupposes a *prior political and ethical option in the light of the gospel,* for the poor: liberation theology has chosen the option of evaluating social reality from the viewpoint of the poor, of reflecting theologically from the cause of the poor and acting for the liberation of the poor. This is a political option because the theologian has a place in a specific social context, alongside the oppressed; it is ethical, because it arises out of an indignation, an ethical indignation at the scandal of poverty; and it is in the light of the gospel because it finds its most profound motivation in the gospel (Matt.25.35-46), according to which the poor are the eschatological criterion of salvation or damnation.[39]

This prior option determines the 'social context', the place where the theologian does theology, and this in turn 'interferes' with the 'epistemological context', with the way in which the theologian does theology. The 'interference' excludes both the lack of relationship between theory and practice and the existence of a direct relationship, in that the logic of science is not the logic of praxis; the 'interference' of the social context in the epistemological or theoretical context indicates an indirect relationship in the sense that the social context makes possible a corresponding theological discourse: 'what to do' becomes the object of 'what to think'. Under the pressure of this prior option, with such a configuration, the theology of liberation is a theology *desde* and *sobre*, from and about praxis, theology understood strictly as a second act.

2. The theology of liberation uses a socio-analytical mediation. Theology has always used philosophical methods or a philosophical mediation (the totality of conceptual instruments considered by philosophy) in its reflection and has given them a favoured place; one need only think of Platonism in the patristic period, Aristotelianism in the scholastic period or the modern theme of the transcendental in the theology of Rahner; by

9

contrast the theology of liberation, which begins from praxis and aims at praxis, uses the social sciences and gives priority to socio-analytical mediation.[40]

It does not follow from this that the theology of liberation excludes philosophical mediation. The theology of liberation is not the whole of theology; it is a T^2 (secondary theology) which presupposes a T^1 (primary theology); in other words, all the previous discourse has as its presupposition Christian revelation and salvation, where a multiple and varied mediation continues to be at work: philology, history and philosophy. But in the specific quality of its discourse the theology of liberation gives priority to socio-analytical mediation. The link between theology and praxis acts through the framework of socio-analytical mediation: 'Theological humanism can no longer occupy... the —whole— space of the theological problematic.'[41]

But what socio-analytical mediation? That depends in the last instance on the prior option chosen by the liberation theologian: 'A correct response may be given to this question in the form of a reference to the practices of engaged Christian communities. We may then say that the solution is given *in actu*, in the ethico-political option that these communities have made in the name of the Christian faith.' And again: 'Suffering and struggling side by side with non-Christians and the most alert of scientists, these Christians have resolutely chosen a conflictual reading of the reality that is theirs. And they have done so on the basis of criteria furnished by their very faith, in articulation with analyses of the sciences of the social.'[42]

3. The theology of liberation calls for a renewed use of hermeneutical mediation; it does not interpret scripture and the sources of the Christian tradition in the abstract, but on the basis of a specific political and social situation, read through socio-analytical mediation. It is by hermeneutical mediation that the social reading of reality is transformed into theological reading of the same reality: 'The process of theological articulation consists in this: to transform, with the help of the properly theological concept of "salvation", the sociological concept of

10

"liberation" in such a way as to produce a theological proposition such as "liberation is salvation".'[43] And this is the pattern according to which hermeneutical mediation and socio-analytical mediation is articulated.

For Juan Luis Segundo, the hermeneutical circle does not function in academic theology. Academic theology infers its perennial responses from the content of revelation, considered from an atemporal perspective, and applies them to the human situation. By contrast, the theology of liberation reintroduces the hermeneutical circle: it begins from a specific situation, from which current questions arise, and puts these questions to the revelation. The revelation, interrogated in this way, provides a response which illuminates the individual and social situation of the person putting the questions. This gives rise to the theology of liberation: by restoring the hermeneutical circle it frees theology from false universalism. In this way the theology of liberation also brings about a 'liberation of theology', to take the title of a book by this Uruguayan theologian.[44]

4. The theology of liberation is biassed towards praxis and calls for a consistent practical and pastoral mediation following on the social analysis made and the theological reading given. The prior acceptance of socio-analytical mediation and hermeneutical mediation ensures a correct articulation of the relationship between theology and praxis: if it used only the socio-analytical mediation, theology would turn into sociologism; if it used only the hermeneutical mediation it would turn into theologism; if it used only the practical and pastoral mediation it would turn into pastoral pragmatism. The theology of liberation is constructed on the basic option for the poor and in the mutual articulation of these three mediations. The three mediations correspond to the tripartite scheme of analysis of the facts, theological reflection and pastoral suggestions; this can also be found in the church documents which follow the line of liberation theology.[45]

In substance, the novelty of liberation theology consists in the acceptance of socio-analytical mediation within theological discourse: this involves a restructuring of hermeneutical

11

mediation and practical pastoral mediation, mediations already operating in traditional theological discourse.

So just as the assumption of socio-analytical mediation depends on a prior option in favour of the oppressed and is directed towards a praxis of liberation, so the social analysis favoured is not of a functional type (society seen as an organic whole) which would lead to a reformist practice, but of a dialectical type (society as a complex of forces in tension), which leads to a praxis of liberation.

In this context the assumption of socio-analytical mediation usually involves the critical utilization of conceptual instruments drawn from the Marxist tradition: 'After Marx, theology may no longer put in parentheses the material conditions of existence, thus "mystifying" the realities of unjust situations. Theological statements about social reality have credibility only in the position of a second word, that is, after they have done justice to conditions as they are.'[46] And with this we can identify one of the key points of the new theological project.

The theology of liberation is not a unitary block; it is possible to identify different currents within it which on the basis of a careful analysis[47] can be reduced to four: 1. theology on the basis of the pastoral praxis of the church: it is a theology of liberation in the broad sense, aimed at the pastoral and spiritual aspects of liberation and not so much at the cultural and socio-political aspects; 2. theology on the basis of the praxis of the Latin American peoples (represented by some Argentinian theologians like Lucio Gera and Juan Carlos Scannone):[48] it gives priority to the cultural aspects of the popular ethos and not so much to the socio-political aspects; 3. theology on the basis of historical praxis: this is the current which fully realizes the description which I have given above and which includes the main representatives of the theology of liberation; in the context of integral liberation this stresses the relevance of the social and political aspects of liberation; 4. theology on the basis of the praxis of revolutionary groups: what is predominant here is discussion of the political revolutionary action of Christian groups.

12

Liberation theology and European theology

From 1975 on (i.e. from after the first Detroit conference), Latin American liberation theology has been associated with black theology and with feminist theology, which also understand themselves as liberation theologies;[49] from 1976 (the conference in Dar-es-Salaam, Tanzania)[50] liberation theology has initiated a process of liaisons with the theologies of the Third World and has thus come to be shaped as 'a theological expression of the Third World'.[51]

In modern times Christian theology had been predominantly European with an extension across the North Atlantic and into the academic world; but the new theology came into being in Latin America, on the geo-political periphery, and was written by theologians committed to the struggle for the liberation of their continent. However, with polemical lucidity it did not present itself as 'Latin American theology', as if only European theology were, or should continue to be, 'the' theology of the universal church, but presented itself as a question and a challenge to the conscience of all Christians, as prophetic testimony to the universal church, as the contribution of Latin America to a truly 'catholic' theology.

In one of the most illuminating pages in all contemporary theological literature Gutiérrez has identified the difference in commitment between the theology which is cultivated in the European sphere and the new theological project developed in Latin America: 'It seems that a good deal of contemporary theology has begun from the challenge posed by the unbeliever. The unbeliever puts our religious world in question, requiring of it a purification and a profound renewal. Bonhoeffer accepted the challenge and gave incisive expression to the question which underlies many contemporary theological works: how do we proclaim God in a world which has come of age? But in a continent like Latin America the challenge does not come principally from the non-believer, but from the non-person, i.e. the person who is not recognized as human by the dominant social order: the

13

poor, the exploited, the one who is systematically and legally despoiled of his human nature, the one who hardly feels human. The non-person first of all puts in question not so much our religious world as our economic, social, political and cultural world; therefore all revolutionary transformation draws on the same basis of a de-humanized society. So the question is not so much how to speak of God in a world come of age, as how to proclaim the Father in an inhuman world, the implications of what it means to tell the non-person that he or she is a child of God.'[52] The difference in the audience, i.e. the difference in context, determines the difference in the basis of liberation theology from that of European or North Atlantic theology. We shall try to locate the relationships and the differences more precisely.

At the beginning of this new course, in his *A Theology of Human Hope* (1969) – the title of which was meant as polemic against Jürgen Moltmann's *Theology of Hope* (1964), Rubem Alves was developing a critique of the language of contemporary European theology, particularly in Barth, Bultmann and Moltmann. His criticism was aimed at showing how theological language had hitherto always referred to metaphysical and meta-historical realities, and it marked the birth of new communities of Christians inspired by a vision and a passion for human liberation, for whom theological language was historical language. Although the language of the 'theology of hope' also acted as a corrective to dialectical and existentialist theology, it still produced a 'tangent to history'.[53]

The theology of liberation immediately sought to differentiate itself from the so-called theology of revolution, which was first formulated in the context of the 'Church and Society' conference of the World Council of Churches in Geneva in 1966. It was the resumption, in a new world-political situation, of a theme already expressed at the beginning of the century by the North American theologian of the social gospel, Walter Rauschenbusch, who in his first work, *Christianity and the Social Crisis* (1907), already wrote: 'Christian ascetism called the world evil and abandoned it. Humanity is waiting for a Christian revolution which will call the world evil and change it', and by the Swiss theologians of Religious Socialism like Hermann Kutter and Leonhard Ragaz. At Geneva the theme of revolution was introduced into the ecumenical debate by the North American theologian Richard Shaull, who had vast experience of the problems of Latin America. He was not seeking to develop a systematic theology of revolution but to raise the problem of the relationship between Christian vocation and the participation of Christians in the revolutionary struggle. For Shaull, the Christian vocation can nourish an authentic revolutionary vocation.

European theologians like Helmut Gollwitzer and Jürgen Moltmann made their contribution to the debate on the relationship between Christianity and revolution. Gollwitzer connected the concept of revolution with that of the kingdom of God: 'The "kingdom of God" is the content of a promise which revolutionizes the present. Moltmann associated the eschatological theme of hope, which opens up the horizons of the future, with the apocalyptic theme of the 'break' with the past: the future goes against the past by breaking with it; indeed, 'the symbols and the images of the Bible stress the discontinuity, the condemnation, the end of the world and the outbreak of something completely new'.

Hugo Assmann quickly pointed out that such a 'general' theology of revolution became generic, abstract, because it went round the theme, discussed theological problems of context (kingdom of God, apocalyptic) and 'moved away from the facts'; it was not – to make things more specific in terms of the language of the theology of liberation – reflection as a 'second act'.[54]

The theme was taken up in the lengthy books by Joseph Comblin, *Théologie de la revolution* (1970) and *Théologie de la pratique révolutionnaire* (1974), which remain the most complete systematic treatment of the theology of revolution.[55] For the Belgian theologian, living in Latin America, since with the arrival on the world scene of the proletarian nations of the Third World humanity finds itself in a revolutionary situation, it is necessary to develop a theology of revolution. Comblin, who later came increasingly close to the theology of liberation without ever identifying with it, defined the relationship between the two theologies as follows: 'On the one hand liberation is broader than revolution, which represents only one dimension of it. On the other hand, if liberation is understood as a process of emancipation from the imperial domination of the developed nations, it can only be conceived of in the context of a world revolution. It is impossible for Latin America to change without there also being a complete change throughout the world society of the industrialized nations: no liberation is possible in the form of a new "war of independence"; no nation can ever liberate itself; it is necessary for the change to be universal. In this sense a Latin American liberation is one of the aspects of world revolution in modern society which is a unitary society embracing the totality of nations'.[56] At all events, even with these acculturations of the theology of revolution in the Latin American context, like that outlined by Comblin, the theologians of liberation have constantly confirmed that they stand apart from the so-called theology of revolution. As Leonardo Boff recently wrote: 'This theology did not arise, as might be supposed, in Latin America. Rather, it consists of reflections arising out of the sphere of the rich societies, as it were "a way of compensating for the emptiness of historical function which has been noted by Christians".'[57]

As is well known, between 1965 and 1968 the programme of a political theology began to develop in Europe as a result of the work of Johann Baptist Metz; he was soon joined by other theologians, including Moltmann himself, who planned in this way to give concrete expression to his theology of hope. The Latin American theology of liberation and European political theology come together in what could be defined as the political shift in theology in the 1960s, but these are two theological models with very different aspects. First of all the two theologies are almost contemporaneous (political theology arose directly out of Metz's lecture at the Toronto Congress in the summer of 1967; and as we have already noted, the theology of liberation arose

16

out of the lecture by Gutiérrez at the pastoral meeting at Chimbote in summer 1968). They grew up in different contexts, and therefore one cannot derive the theology of liberation from political theology, regarding the former as a 'Latin American form of political theology', as has been done in over-hasty reconstructions not only in Europe but also in Latin America. Moreover these two theologies have been in tension from the beginning, as is demonstrated by the bitter discussion at the 1973 Geneva symposium organized by the World Council of Churches[58] and by the polemical 'Open Letter of 1975' from Jürgen Moltmann to the Argentinian theologian José Míguez Bonino, author of *Doing Theology in a Revolutionary Situation*.[59]

According to the analysis made by Xosé Miguélez,[60] on the presupposition that one of the basic principles of Christian faith is the vocation of human beings to be children of God, Christian theological discourse with its themes moves on four levels: (*a*) the prior acceptance of the free gift of God in a filial attitude and in thanksgiving; (*b*) the welcoming of the gift pledges one to bring about brotherhood with other human beings. But the obligation to achieve brotherhood can also be seen as a historical project which needs to be realized. And in its turn this involves (*c*) a critical attitude to the given situation in that this is always inadequate for the project; and (*d*) the need to construct the new project, which also uses the mediation of a radical analysis of the causes of the historical situation that are to be overcome. If a pre-critical theology keeps to the themes of the first two levels, (*a*) and (*b*), political theology also takes up the themes of level (*c*), which sees praxis as an imperative of faith, while the theology of liberation goes so far as also to take in level (*d*), which sees praxis as a proof of faith. According to this analysis, political theology and the theology of liberation converge in both presenting themselves as a theology of praxis, but the theology of liberation differs from political theology in that it is shaped as a specific and radical form of the theology of praxis.[61]

Gutiérrez has deepened the methodological intuition of his essay 'Praxis of Liberation, Theology and Proclamation' (1975) in other essays brought together in Part IV of *The Power of the Poor in History* (1979),[62] in which he explicitly deals with the theme of the confrontation between the theology of liberation and 'progressive' European theology, of which political theology is the spearhead. These are two profoundly different theologies, in that they move on different horizons and in different contexts and try to face different challenges: if progressive theology faces the challenge of critical rationality and individual freedom in the context of a society forged by the middle class, the theology of liberation is discussion with 'those who are absent from history', who in Latin America are involved in becoming the historical subject of a process of popular liberation, and this means 'calling into question first of all the economic, social and political order that oppresses them and marginalizes them, and of course the ideology that is brought in to justify this domination'.[63] The theologian from Lima accuses European theology, including that progressive theology which seeks to deal with the problems posed by the modern world, of not bringing into the discussion the concrete historical basis on which the modern world is fashioned. With reference to the progressive theology of Bonhoeffer's 'world come of age', Gutiérrez writes: 'Taken up as he is with the fascist enemy and its attacks on liberal society from the rear, Bonhoeffer was less sensitive to the world of injustice on which that society was built.'[64] The difference between the two theologies arises, in the last analysis, from a political cleavage: 'The exploited classes, despised ethnic groups and marginalized cultures are the historical subject of a new understanding of the faith.'[65]

The profound methodological analysis of Clodovis Boff's *Theology and Praxis* (1978) has identified the structural elements in the discourse of the theology of liberation, indicating the epistemological peculiarities in its adoption of socio-analytical mediation. Socio-analytical mediation is necessary for reading reality, which in the case of the relationship between theory and praxis is social. But socio-analytical mediation can be ignored or taken up in the wrong way: 'theologism' ignores it by substituting theology for socio-analytical mediation, to which it attributes

18

everything, as if theology could pronounce on everything without the mediation of science; however, 'bilingualism' assumes socio-analytical mediation, but without articulating it in theological discourse. In the analysis by Clodovis Boff, political theology practises a kind of bilingualism which takes two synoptic readings of reality, arriving at vague formulae like 'faith involves politics', 'the gospel also has a political dimension', 'the church also has a mission of a social kind' in which socio-analytical mediation is certainly accepted, but simply juxtaposed to the theological data without a real articulation capable of conditioning hermeneutical mediation and practical pastoral mediation. This is a bilingualism which at times also takes the form of a 'semantic mixture' of two linguistic genres, sociological and theological.[66]

The difficulties, both political and ecclesiastical, in which the theology of liberation has gradually found itself, have led to a transformation of the initial tension and polemic between political theology and the theology of liberation into a constructive confrontation which has just begun, from different positions. In it the diversity is provided in the last analysis by a political rupture (Gutiérrez), by the diversity of the 'social context' (C.Boff) in which political theologians from Europe and North America on the one hand and the Latin American liberation theologians on the other are working, only converging in different geopolitical contexts in the search for the link between faith, theology and praxis.

2 · Themes and Topics of Research in Liberation Theology

As well as having introduced a new way of doing theology, as a reflection which begins from praxis and is focussed on praxis, the theology of liberation has developed some themes and topics of research in an original way, in particular in christology and ecclesiology.

Jesus Christ Liberator

In the christological field Leonardo Boff – who writes from a Teilhardian perspective[1] – has developed a first synthesis of the new perspective of liberation in *Jesus Christ Liberator* (1972).[2] This christology is characterized (*a*) by the primacy of anthropology over ecclesiology: in Latin America it is not the church which is the focus of attention, but human beings, whom it is called to raise up and humanize; (*b*) by the primacy of the utopian over the factual: the kingdom is anticipated in history and the new man is in process of coming to birth; the reconciliation promised and realized in Christ is a completion of the human realization; (*c*) by the primacy of the critical over the dogmatic element through the need to discern the nucleus of liberation in the Christian message; (*d*) by the primacy of the social over the personal with a stress on the secular and liberating dimensions of the message of Christ; (*e*) by the primacy of orthopraxis over orthodoxy with a stress on the praxological element of the message of Christ.[3]

In his attempt to express the reality of Jesus of Nazareth in the present situation in Latin America Boff suggests the christological

20

title of Liberator: 'Perhaps a suitable description of Jesus would be Liberator of a consciousness oppressed by sin and by all alienations and Liberator of the sad human condition in its relationships with the world, the other, and God'.[4] In fact Jesus announces the kingdom of God in his preaching as 'a new order of things', as 'the revolution and the total, global and structural transfiguration of the reality of our world', as 'the utopia of absolute liberation' which calls for anticipatory realizations in history; the *acta et facta* of Jesus, in other words his praxis, are to be understood as a historicization of the specific meaning of the kingdom of God, as the setting in motion of a process of liberation; the conversion to which Jesus calls people indicates the need to give concrete form to the liberation brought about by God; the violent death undergone by Jesus must be explained as a re-action to his liberating action and as the price of God's liberation in the conflictual reality of history;[5] the resurrection of Jesus is the anticipatory irruption of the definite liberation by means of which the *u-topia* of the kingdom becomes *topia* in history; for Christians discipleship becomes the form which gives actuality and specific historicity to God's liberation: 'To follow Jesus is to follow his work, to pursue a cause and to join in his fullness.'[6]

Leonardo Boff has meditated further on these perspectives in formulating the thesis: 'Although the kingdom is not this-worldly in origin (it has its origin in God), it is present in our midst, manifesting itself in processes of liberation.'[7] If he is asked how total liberation (= salvation) is related to partial liberations (on the economic, poitical and social level), Boff replies by indicating four models of relationship: (*a*) the Chalcedonian model: as in Christ divinity and humanity are related in such a way as to form a dual unity without division or separation, but also without confusion or mutation, so eschatological salvation intrinsically includes historical liberations: 'Jesus, our salvation, is also our liberator'; 'eschatological salvation goes through historical liberations'; 'salvation and liberation are realized without division and without separation, but also without confusion and without mutation from one to the other'; (b) the sacramental model: just as, according to the principle of sacramentality, grace is mediated (= sacrament) by a reality of this world to which it is joined, so historical liberations are not dissociated from salvation, even if salvation is not just realized in historical liberations; (c) the agapic model: according to the Christian concept of love there is an identification between love of God and love of neighbour, to the degree that the one who loves his or her neighbour loves God; just as God is to be encountered in the neighbour, so salvation is to be encountered in historical liberation; (d) the anthropological model: the unity and difference of the two principles (body and soul) which make up the human being serve to illuminate the unity and the difference between historical liberations and eschatological salvation.

However, the most developed christological sketch in the perspective of the theology of liberation is that put forward by the Spanish theologian Jon Sobrino, from El Salvador, in his *Christology at the Crossroads*, the original Spanish sub-title of which is 'An outline on the basis of discipleship of the historical Jesus', and which the author presents as an ecclesial, historical and trinitarian christology.[8]

First of all it is (a) an ecclesial christology, in the sense that in analogy to the christologies of the New Testament, where Christ is thought of originally in terms of the situation and praxis of the first Christian communities, it is meant to reflect the life and praxis of the church communities in Latin America and overall to make possible and to give sense to this life and this praxis. In other words, it is a christological reflection understood as a second act which presupposes a well determined ecclesial and social context – the experience of the encounter with Jesus in the poor and a practice of liberation – that demands a particular use of theological understanding. So it is ecclesial christology, in the sense that it is *contextualized* by the experience of the church of the poor to which it seeks to give expression and which it seeks to accompany with reflection. Therefore the christology of liberation – as Sobrino calls it – does not claim to be the whole of christology, nor is it its task to deal with all historical and systematic questions, but it is aware of representing a creative hermeneutical perspective which is a corrective of all christological reflection; being contextualized 'from Latin America', it calls for a demanding and inescapable contextualization starting from discipleship of Jesus: 'Discipleship of Jesus is the primary context of all Christian theological epistemology.'[9]

Moreover it is (b) a historical christology, which considers the New Testament fundamentally as a history and only secondarily as doctrine, and which arrives at the Christ of faith through the Jesus of history, in other words through the specific story of Jesus considered in its totality. In it his praxis takes on a particular role. In this sense the christology of liberation finds a place in the process of the historicization of the event of Christ which is specific to contemporary christological reflection, but in its own mode. The christology of liberation seeks to practise a 'real historicization' of Jesus in the sense that the 'historical Jesus' which represents its starting point is understood as the 'story of Jesus'.

As a historical christology, the christology of liberation is a christology 'from below', but not precisely in the sense of Pannenberg's christology, which in theory and practice is a christology from below beginning not from dogmatic formulations but from the fact of the resurrection, which is historical and at the same time incomparable (with other historical facts): the resurrection analysed in its proleptic structure, but in such a way as to begin from the specific history of Jesus considered in its totality, which includes his resurrection as a decisive element yet which in the last instance calls for the praxis of Jesus as service for the kingdom: 'The most historical thing about the historical Jesus is his praxis, in other words, his activity to work actively on the surrounding reality and to transform it in the particular direction which is sought, in the direction of the kingdom of God... For us, therefore, the history of the historical Jesus is in the first place an invitation (and a demand) to follow his praxis: in the language of Jesus, to follow him on a mission.'[10] The rediscovery of the historical Jesus as the story of Jesus does not, however, put the christology of liberation alongside liberal theology, which went in search of the true 'life of Jesus'; the christology of liberation is aware that the New Testament narratives are narratives in faith which do not allow the reconstruction of a biography of Jesus in the technical sense of modern historiography, and moreover because of its historical contextualization the liberal contrast between the Jesus of history and the Christ of church dogma is quite extraneous to it. The christology of liberation is not in search of the true 'life of Jesus' in order to criticize the dogma of the church; it means to rediscover the story of Jesus in all its historical depth in order to rediscover christological dogma as a doxological formula to be verified in praxis. The christology of liberation theologizes historically, but at the same time with a dialectical procedure unknown to liberal theology and to all Jesuology which historicizes in a *theologizing* way.

In this sense the christology of liberation is also different from the recent 'materialistic readings' of the Bible (Belo, Clévenot) which interpret the Gospel narratives of the life of Jesus in terms of praxis, but do not go on to elaborate a christology proper. A third connotation arises out of this.

(*c*) The christology of liberation is not only a historical christology but also a trinitarian christology, in which the Father is the ultimate horizon, the Son the definitive example of how to correspond to the Father, and life in the Spirit of Jesus the specific form of being Christian. It begins from the historical Jesus, but puts him in the totality of the mystery of Christ and the trinitarian God. It is the methodological movement of christology from below, which the christology of liberation performs in following its pattern of reflection.

Jesus does not announce himself, nor simply God, but the kingdom of God, and with his activity of liberation he puts himself at the service of the kingdom and makes it present. Jesus is seen constantly in his constitutive relationship with the Father and with his kingdom. The specific history of Jesus is a way towards

24

the Father and is the historical version of the eternal Sonship of the Son. Through his history, with his faith and trust in the Father, with obedience to his mission, in his death and resurrection, Jesus 'reveals to us... the way of the Son, the way one becomes Son of God'.[11] This is one of the phrases in Sobrino's christology which has caused perplexity. Sobrino has explained more precisely what he means on several occasions, asserting that this formulation is not in any way meant to weaken the ontological reality of the divine nature of Christ, but only to demonstrate how the divinity of Christ, his divine Sonship, 'shows itself to us'.[12]

It follows from this that to confess that Jesus is the Son of God is to make effective a story of filiation; the story of Jesus continues in the discipleship of Jesus: 'The most urgent task of christology is to reposition the path and course of believers so that their lives can be a continuing, advancing discipleship, a following of Jesus, and hence a process of concrete filiation as his life was.'[13]

In Jesus there appears the true way, the way to the Father, the way to the God of the kingdom. And the God of the kingdom is the God of life: a God who is the living one and who gives life, as opposed to the idols which give death. In Latin America the problem of distinguishing the true God from false deities, faith in the true God from idolatry, is acute; if European theology is confronted above all with the problem of atheism, Latin American theology of liberation is confronted above all with the abuse, with the manipulation, of the name of God, with idolatry.[14]

Discipleship in the steps of Jesus becomes the basic moral demand, the general paradigm of Christian existence, of life in the Spirit, but 'we are dealing with a messianic conception of discipleship rather than a christological conception in the strict sense'.[15] Discipleship keeps to Jesus to the degree that he proclaims the kingdom and makes it present: it is discipleship of Jesus in the sense of 'making the kingdom'. Praxis becomes an expression of specific orthodoxy; it is a proof of orthodoxy and doxology: 'Christian life as a whole can be described as the following of Jesus. That is the most original and all-embracing reality, far more so than cultic worship and orthodoxy. Rather than being opposed to these latter, however, the following of Jesus integrates and crystallizes them.'[16]

To describe christological reflection from Latin America, Sobrino distinguishes two elements in the process of the Enlightenment: the demand of critical rationality (Kant) and the demand of transforming praxis (Marx). European theology (and christology) is to be measured by the problems inherent in the first element of the Enlightenment, but only the theology of liberation takes up the problems posed by the second demand: 'History indicates that European christology has been more interested in demonstrating the truth of Christ before the bar of reason, though more recent political christologies do move in a somewhat different direction. By contrast christological reflection in Latin America seeks to respond to the second phase of the Enlightenment noted above. It seeks to show how the truth of Christ is capable of transforming a single world into the kingdom of God.'[17]

To sum up, the main characteristics of the christology of liberation[18] are: (a) stress on the *historical* dimension of the salvation brought by Christ: eschatological salvation goes through historical liberations, even if it cannot be identified with them; (b) stress on discipleship, which brings into play a practical hermeneutic that interprets not so much in order to understand (a function which always remains necessary and important) as above all to put into practice: christology of liberation is christology of discipleship; and finally, (c) the use of an 'epistemological suspicion'[19] which seeks to react to the various incorrect presentations of Christ which can easily lend themselves to an ideological use on the part of those who hold power in Latin America. These include, in particular: the Christ reduced to a 'sublime abstraction'; the Christ presented undialectically as 'universal reconciliation'; the 'absolutizing of Christ' in which the relation between Jesus and the kingdom of God which is essential for him is lost; the conquering Christ of the christology of domination; or the conquered Christ of the christology of resignation:[20] 'So we have the abstract Christ, the impartial Christ and the power-wielding Christ. These are the religious symbols that those in power need. These are the symbols that they have used, wittingly or unwittingly, to maintain the Latin American continent in its present state';[21] '...the image of a liberating Jesus is very different from Christ the heavenly monarch of dogmatic piety or the conquered and suffering Christ of popular piety.'[22]

The church of the poor

A great deal of reflection is being done in Latin America in the area of ecclesiology in an effort to interpret (as a second act) the new pastoral praxis of communities which are concerned with liberation. The Chilean theologian Ronaldo Muñoz has analysed about 300 church documents produced in Latin America in the five years immediately following the Council, 1965-1970, and has spoken – as the title of his study indicates – of the emergence of 'a new awareness of the church in Latin America'.[23]

The Latin American bishops did not take part in the Council of Trent (1545-1563) because the Spanish crown had succeeded in obtaining a dispensation for them, giving the length of the journey as the reason; their participation in the First Vatican Council (1869-1870) had been small (there were only sixty-five bishops there from Latin America) and insignificant; although far more bishops took part in Vatican II (there were 601 bishops and official *periti*, amounting to 22% of the whole Council) it was insignificant,[24] to such a degree that the Latin American church present at the Council could be called a 'church of silence'.[25] It was with the second conference of the Latin American episcopate at Medellín – held in 1968, only three years after the conclusion of the Council, and described by contemporary accounts as 'the little council of Medellín'[26] – that the new awareness of the church found expression.

According to Pablo Richard the Medellín conference amounted to a 'reinterpretation of the Council' and not just an application: 'Medellín did not apply Vatican II, but reinterpreted it in the light of the reality of Latin America... If the synods III of Mexico and Lima in the sixteenth century were the application in Latin America of the Council of Trent, and if the plenary Latin American Council of 1899 was the application of Vatican I, the Medellín conference was not the application of Vatican II but its interpretation in terms of the realities of the history of Latin America.'[27] According to the reconstruction by Leonardo Boff,[28] the Medellín conference and the theology of liberation represent a 'creative review' of the Council by the church in Latin America. Vatican II can be seen as the goal of a long process in which faith sought to respond to the challenges of the modern era. With the conciliar constitution *Gaudium et spes* the Catholic Church passed from a relationship of hostility to the modern world – which found expression in the *Syllabus* of Pius IX – to a 'new spirit of solidarity of the new Christians with people of today, especially with the poor and all the oppressed'. But the Council had also generalized above all on the topic of poverty, in that it had not produced in-depth analyses of the mechanisms which generate the poverty of the poor. In Latin America the Council did not function only as a goal, but also as a starting point for a new awareness of being the church. According to this analysis the Latin American church produced a 'creative review' of the Council in the light of the reality of Latin America, in the perspective of the poor: solidarity with people of today becomes solidarity with the poor; the church which lives out this solidarity is the church of the poor, and the theology which follows this route and this process and reflects on it is the theology of liberation.

Ecclesiology in the context of the theology of liberation[29] is in line with post-Vatican ecclesiologies, which have operated a kind of ecclesiological decentralization, in that they have shown that the church does not exist for itself but in terms of the world to which it announces salvation. But which world? And what salvation? The post-Vatican ecclesiologies generally raise the problem of the needs of the church in secular society which tends to marginalize it; the ecclesiology of liberation, on the other hand, raises the problem of mission and the options of the church in a world marked out by poverty and injustice. This gives it some distinctive characteristics.

28

(*a*) The terms of the church's relationship change: it is not with the secular world come of age nor with the world intent on progress, but with the world of poverty and injustice, and this leads to making salvation historically specific. The church is the sign and the instrument of this salvation. The ecclesiology of liberation understands the church as 'the sacrament of integral liberation',[30] in this way seeking to overcome supernaturalist reductionism, which reduces salvation to the supernatural sphere; ecclesiocentric reductionism, which in practice identifies the church with the kingdom; and eschatological reductionism, according to which salvation has a purely other-worldly character. Thus the ecclesiology of liberation rejects the accusation of reductionism: 'It neutralizes the accusation, whether direct or veiled, that the theology of liberation offers only a social and political salvation; such a reduction in no way turns it into Marxism; what the theology of liberation affirms is that the history of salvation is not the history of salvation if it does not affect the social and political dimension. That is its essence, even if it is not its totality.'[31] The church is the *historical* sacrament of liberation in the twofold sense that in its reality as church it is an effect of the salvation which is being realized in history, and altogether, in its mission, it should signify dynamically in history, to the world of injustice and oppression, the salvation which is given it: 'The church realizes its historical salvific sacramentality by proclaiming and realizing the kingdom of God in history. Its fundamental praxis consists in the realization of the kingdom of God in history, in making the kingdom of God real in history.'[32] From this perspective, the novelty of the ecclesiology of liberation consists in stressing the *historicity* of the saving sacramentality of the church and in assuming – in a definite situation of domination and oppression – liberation as a historical form of salvation.

(*b*) The ecclesiology of liberation has, moreover, achieved in an original way the rediscovery of the biblical category of the people of God which has been endorsed in Vatican II and in the post-Vatican ecclesiologies. But if in European ecclesiology this has mostly amounted to a demand for declericalization, in the

29

sense that the church as the new people of God must take historical form in such a way that it is true that 'we are all the church' (Hans Küng), or even, in accordance with the understanding of political theology of the transition from a 'church present for the people' to a 'church of the people' (Johann Baptist Metz), in the ecclesiology of liberation the need has been felt, in order to clarify the liberating mission of the church, to 'fill the idea of the "people of God" with sociological reality in the light of the question "Who is the people?" '.[33]

In his clear essay, 'Theology from the Underside of History', Gustavo Gutiérrez has written: 'In recent years it has seemed more and more clear to many Christians that, if the church wishes to be faithful to the God of Jésus Christ, it must become aware of itself from underneath, from among the poor of this world, the exploited classes, despised ethnic groups, and marginalized cultures. It must descend into the hell of this world, into communion with the misery, injustice, struggles, and hopes of the wretched of the earth – for "of such is the kingdom of heaven"... To be born, to be reborn, as church, from below, from among them, today means to die, in a concrete history of oppression and complicity with oppression. In this ecclesiological approach, which takes up one of the central themes of the Bible, Christ is seen as the Poor One identified with the oppressed and plundered of the world. Here new paths open wide, for this is what is called the underside of history.'[34] Jon Sobrino has also spoken, with reference to the ecclesial and ecclesiological newness of the church of the poor, of the 'resurrection of the true church', to quote the original title of his collection of essays on ecclesiology.[35]

The ecclesiology of liberation has developed the image of the church of the poor, to be understood not only in the sense that it must be a poor church in order to fulfil its mission, nor mainly in the sense that the church must be preoccupied with the poor and be for the poor, but in the sense that it must understand itself and act from (*desde*) the poor: 'The response is relatively simple at the theological level: The Spirit of Jesus is in the poor and, with them as his point of departure, he re-creates the whole church... For this profound reason I maintain that the Church of the poor is not a Church for the poor but a Church that must be formed on the basis of the poor and that must find in them the principle of its structure, organization and mission...This means that the poor are the authentic *theological source* for understanding Christian truth and practice and therefore the constitution of the Church.'[36]

The poor are a theological locus, not in the classical sense of a 'source', for attaining the truth of faith, but in the dynamic sense of a place where there is manifested in a special way the presence of the God of Jesus Christ (to begin with, a hidden and disconcerting presence, which then becomes a prophetic presence, in that it makes a proclamation and a denunciation, and finally an apocalyptic presence, in that it demands the end of the time of oppression and prepares for the irruption of a new time): a place where discipleship of Jesus – in accordance with Matt.25 – becomes more urgent, and where therefore deeper reflection in faith and an authentic Christian theology is made possible.[37]

The ecclesiology of liberation also speaks of a 'church which grows out of the people', but in making this statement it does not mean to say that the people are the main source of the church; the church arises *desde el pueblo por el Espiritu*, in other words it rises, or rises again, or renews itself *from* the people *by the power of* the Spirit: the movement from above always precedes the movement from below; nor is this meant to be the affirmation of an anarchical tendency which excludes the hierarchy and the ministers; it is meant, rather, to stress the process of renewal in action in Latin America of a church which is close to the people, which becomes incarnate among ordinary people and which in this way makes itself poorer, more brotherly, more prophetic, more stamped by the values of the kingdom. The church 'grows out of the people' by making itself the 'church of the poor'.[38]

It is in this context that the controversial expression *Iglesia popular* appears, a term which has often been taken up and made more profound.[39] The Final Statement from Puebla made it more precise in some respects. 'The problem of the "people's Church", the Church born of the people, has various aspects. The first obstacle is readily surmounted if it is interpreted as a Church that is trying to incarnate itself in the ranks of the common people on our continent, and that therefore arises out of their response in faith to the Lord. This rules out the seeming denial of a basic truth: i.e., that the Church always arises from a first initiative "from above", from the Spirit who raises it up and from the Lord who convokes it. Nevertheless the appellation seems to be quite unfortunate. The "people's Church" seems to be something distinct from some "other" Church – the latter being identified with the "official" or "institutional" Church and accused of being "alienating". This suggests a division within the bosom of the Church and seems to imply an unacceptable denial of the hierarchy's functions' (no.263).

The ecclesiology of liberation has thus been called on to make itself more precise.[40] The 'people's church' cannot be formed as an alternative church to the institutional church, because the epithet 'people's' here does not have a theological value but a sociological one, as in the case of expressions like 'national church' or 'popular Catholicism'; the term 'people's' does not denote a church which is alternative to the institutional church but that part of the one institutional church, the one people of God, which has chosen and lives out the preferential option for the poor and which practises a liberating evangelization.[41] So the 'people's church' does not represent a narrowing of the universality of the church but the church as the people of God taking specific historical form in the situation of Latin America, even if there are clearly tensions and contradictions, not in the institutional church *per se*, but in a certain way of being the church: 'There is a certain tension, and sometimes opposition, between a type of Church that prolongs its incarnation in the ruling bourgeois culture, with the interests vested in this, and this new type of Church which is taking flesh in the popular culture, changing, championing the cause of the people and therefore, rightly, calling itself a popular Church.'[42]

32

(c) The facts that are being tested in the Latin-American church – the participation of believers in the struggles for liberation, the preferential option for the poor on the part of the church, the renewal of the communities from the poor – also have consequences for the structure of the church's ministry. In the first national Brazilian meeting of basic communities, held at Vitória in June 1975, the term 'ecclesiogenesis' appeared several times and was immediately given added depth by Leonardo Boff in his study *Ecclesiogenesis*[43] (1977) and in other essays which were then collected into the controversial volume *Church: Charism and Power*[44] (1981). For Boff, the current ecclesiastical system could be characterized as 'institutional fossilization', the result of a long historical process, lacking in all theological justification and now no longer capable of being corrected with minor reforms. The new reality of the basic communities is characterized by five elements: they arise from the grass-roots, they are born from the word of God, they realize a new way of being the church in terms of community and brotherhood, they celebrate faith and life. This is bringing about a shift in the axis of the church: from a church linked to the ruling class to a church linked to the people and the lower classes (and in this sense a popular church); from a church which acts in a biassed way as a factor of conservation and legitimation to a church which has opted for liberation; from a colonial church for the poor to a church with the poor and of the poor; from a hierarchical church in which all the power is concentrated in the hierarchy to a pneumatological church according to which every Christian has or is a bearer of his or her charisma: 'The charisma does not exclude the hierarchical element but includes it. The charisma is more fundamental to the church than the institutional element. It is the spiritual force which makes the institutions and keeps them alive.'[45]

In short, the ecclesiology of liberation is a critical ecclesiology which above all puts in question the economic and socio-cultural conditions of the life of the church; and as a militant ecclesiology – to take up the original sub-title of Boff's book – to this degree

33

takes shape as the ecclesiological theory of the practices of liberation of the Christian people.

Spirituality, the revision of history writing and the philosophy of liberation

We have traced the essential lines of the christology of discipleship and the militant ecclesiology of the theology of liberation, but other areas should be illustrated and developed. Here I shall limit myself to pointing out the very rich and stimulating literature on the spirituality of liberation, where discipleship of Jesus is seen as a communal way of holiness which does not suppress the personal dimension but gives it its true significance; the vast project of revising the history of the church in Latin America, no longer seen from the perspective of the relationship between church and state, but from the perspective of the poor and the dominated; and finally the broadening of reflection to the point of the search for a philosophy of liberation.

The theology of liberation is not only a theological perspective but above all a spirituality. At the end of the first pages of his *Theology of Liberation* Gutiérrez sees spirituality as one of the functions of theology: 'theology is of necessity both spirituality and rational knowledge'.[46] In its long history, theological reflection has taken a variety of forms; in particular, during the patristic period it was cultivated primarily as knowledge, as an expression of and at the same time as the food of spiritual life; however, during the scholastic period it was seen predominantly as rational knowledge, the result of the encounter between faith and reason, functions which were progressively restricted to the point that in certain manuals they were reduced to a mere exposition and systematization of revealed truth. For Gutiérrez the two functions – sapiential-spiritual and critical-rational – must not be understood in a dialectical sense but as classical forms, as constants which have constantly to be recovered and rearranged in new contexts. Thus from its first beginnings the theology of liberation has sought to weld together wisdom and rational knowledge, spirituality and criticism, life and reflection, but in the new Latin-American perspective which was then being described.[47]

One of the first syntheses to have been put forward is the basic study by Segundo Galilea, *Spirituality of Liberation*, which opens with the assertion: 'So it is possible to speak in Latin America of a theology of liberation and correlatively of a spirituality of liberation. Nowadays there are serious and widespread indications which allow us to affirm how liberating, temporal commitment leads urgently to a rediscovery of faith, contemplation and the values of the gospel'.[48] The spirituality of liberation is characterized by an overcoming of the dualism between contemplation and militancy, between mysticism and commitment: 'There is a pressing need for a synthesis between the "militant" and the "contemplative"...';[49] 'Christian mysticism is mysticism of commitment';[50] 'Christianity realizes the synthesis between the militant and the mystical, the political and the contemplative, overcoming the false antinomy between religious contemplation and militant commitment'.[51]

This is a spirituality which converged with the programme being formulated in Europe at about the same time by Roger Schutz of the Taizé community in his book *Struggle and Contemplation*,[52] taken up and developed in original categories by political theology as 'mysticism and politics of discipleship',[53] but put forward in Latin America with very precise contextualization as 'spirituality of change'.[54]

It is a spirituality of synthesis, the newness of which Leonardo Boff expresses in the programme *contemplativus in liberatione*, as contextualization of the classical programme *contemplativus in actione* (which in turn derives from the *ora et labora* and the *contemplata aliis tradere*), in that here the action is a complex of liberating and transforming practices.[55] For Jon Sobrino the new spirituality which is arising in Latin America takes the form of a political holiness, as 'liberation with the spirit', in that it is a matter of unifying spirit and practice, spirituality and commitment: without the praxis, liberation would be a mere generalization; without the spirit, liberation always remains exposed to the threat of degeneration.[56] It is not an innocuous spirituality, as is dramatically evident from the 'martyrology' of the Latin American church,[57] but a spirituality of persecution and martyrdom.[58]

The Brazilian Jesuit João Batista Libânio[59] has studied the evolution which has been undergone in Latin America by the Ignatian category of discernment with reference to the historical and ecclesial context. The first model of discernment, that prevalent in pre-conciliar theology, asked how the will of God could be discerned in the life of the believer, objectively codified in the commandments and precepts of the church. The second model, which established itself decisively with the spirituality promoted by Vatican II, asks how the divine purpose can be discerned with regard to the personal experience and secular reality in which the believer is situated. The third model is emerging in Latin America, where the basic communities, practising a militant reading of the Bible, are seeking to discern the way indicated by the word of God, taking socio-analytical mediation as an instrument for providing a reading of social reality in which the believing community lives and is called to operate. Here, the basic communities are the privileged place of discernment, where the life of faith and committed militancy is found in a specific form. This third model, peculiar to the spirituality of liberation, does not begin from a codified and objectified theological datum, like the first model, nor does it accord a central place to the personal experience of the Christian who lives in the secular city, like the second model, but has its context in a communal course of liberation.

Gustavo Gutiérrez, who had already stressed the spiritual and sapiential dimensions of the theology of liberation in his major work, returned to the theme in *We Drink from Our Own Wells: The Spiritual Journey of a People*, from which he illustrates the structure and characteristics of the spirituality of liberation.[60] 'To drink from one's own well' is an expression taken from St Bernard's *De consideratione* and seeks to express how in spiritual

36

matters each person should draw on his or her own experience, prompted by the Spirit. In Latin America, the well to drink from is a new type of spirituality, no longer élitist and individualist, practised by few and aimed only at the interior life, but experienced as a common experience and way: 'In our insertion into the process of liberation in which the people of Latin America are now engaged, we live out the gift of faith, hope and charity that makes us disciples of the Lord. This experience is our well. The water that rises out of it continually purifies us and smooths away any wrinkles in our manner of being Christians, at the same time supplying the vital element needed for making new ground fruitful.'[61]

Christian spirituality – as the Peruvian theologian analyses it – is characterized by three elements: first, an encounter with the Lord, understood as a basic spiritual experience from which there derives, as a second element, a life according to the Spirit, which is not to be understood in a spiritualistic sense as living according to the Spirit and against or without the body, but as living in accordance with life, love, peace and justice, which are the great values of the kingdom, and therefore against death; this life according to the Spirit is made real – and this is the third element – in a collective adventure moved by the Spirit, according to the paradigm of the exodus, which finds encounters throughout the history of spirituality: ' "Walking according to the Spirit" is an activity undertaken within a community, a people on the move... When I say that the following of Jesus is a collective adventure I am not, of course, eliminating the personal dimension: on the contrary, I am giving it its authentic meaning as a response to the con-vocation of the Father...'[62] In Latin America it is precisely this communal dimension of spirituality which is affirmed. 'Spirituality is a community enterprise. It is the passage of a people through the solitude and dangers of the desert, as it carves out its own way in the following of Jesus Christ, This spiritual experience is the well from which we must drink. From it we draw the promise of resurrection.'[63] This communal spirituality constitutes the first act, the starting point of that type of reflection which is the theology of liberation, where 'talk about God (theology) comes after the silence of prayer and after commitment'.[64] It therefore follows, according to a profound statement by Gutiérrez, that 'our method is our spirituality'.[65]

The perspective of liberation has led the Argentinian historian Enrique Dussel to formulate a 'Hypothesis for a History of the Church in Latin America', which he has subsequently taken up and developed in his *History of the Church in Latin America*.[66] The theology of liberation is the sign of a reality of the church which is affirmed and which can also function as a hermeneutical key for a new understanding and periodization of the history of the church on the Latin-American sub-continent.

In this perspective the history of the church in Latin America can be sub-divided into three major periods: (*a*) colonial Christianity (1492-1808), the time of the functioning of the *jus patronatus*, granted by the Holy See to Spain and Portugal, which was expressed in the state organization of the 'Council of the Indies', responsible for a time of colonization and mission: 'This ambiguity underlies the whole Portuguese and Spanish enterprise of colonial evangelization and mission colonialization';[67] (*b*) the agony of colonial Christianity and the progressive inauguration of a new order of Christianity (1808-1962), during which the church acted indirectly on society through the Catholic élites; (*c*) and finally, the order of a new period (from 1962) in which the church is confronted with a process of liberation and seeks connections with the popular movements. The theology of liberation is the theological expression which accompanies this new course, and is different from both the colonial theology of the first period and the neo-colonial theology of the second period, but finds a parallel both in the theological and prophetic movement of the first time of conquest and evangelization, exemplified above all in the bishop of the Chiapas, Fra' Bartolomé de las Casas, and the political theology of the time of the national emancipation of the European cities at the beginning of the eighteenth century.[68]

38

The perspective of liberation has also raised questions and problems in the sphere of philosophy. Philosophy begins with the question: is it possible to do theology in an underdeveloped country? The question is then made more precise: is it possible to do theology in a culture which is dependent and dominated? The Peruvian philosopher Augusto Salazar Bondy replied that the reality of domination also denotes cultural domination, 'the culture of domination', and it is precisely this situation which blocks the rise of a Latin American philosophy, even if today it is at least possible to formulate the hypothesis of one. The hypothesis has been taken up and made more profound by a group of scholars, above all from Argentina, among whom mention must be made of the theologian Juan Carlos Scannone and the historian Enrique Dussel.

For Juan Carlos Scannone, a liberation theologian concerned above all with the cultural aspects of the problem, the crisis of the 'liberal historical project' which has functioned in Latin America as 'dependent modernity', opens the way to new cultural possibilities, including philosophical ones: 'It seems that nowadays a new way of thinking is in process of arising in Latin America. Its originality is that of being at the service of the historical process of the liberation of the Latin American people as reflective and critical thought.'[69] If, according to the classical image of Hegel in the Preface to the *Philosophy of Right*, philosophy is the 'owl of Minerva [which] begins its flight at dusk', philosophy in the perspective of liberation can be compared 'to the morning goldfinch (*jilguero de la mañana*) in that it takes on its prophetic mission of indicating the first rays of a new era'.[70] In this sense one can begin to talk of philosophy not only *in* Latin America but *from* (*desde*) Latin America.

However, it is above all Enrique Dussel who has traced the outlines of a philosophy of liberation. For Dussel, philosophical reflection always has deep political roots: 'To be born in New York is not the same thing as to be born at the North Pole or in the Chiapas.'[71] The philosophy of liberation understands itself, from its geographical context, as a philosophy of the periphery,

39

and cannot but appear a barbarous philosophy to the philosophers of the centre.

The philosophy of the centre is a phenomenological ontology which begins from being and circumscribes it in a system; by contrast, the philosophy of the periphery is not an ontology but a metaphysic, in that it takes as its starting point the Other, from outside the system. If the central category of Western philosophy is that of totality, the central category of the philosophy of liberation is that of externality. Externality here is not understood in Hegelian terms as *Ausserlichkeit*, for which existing is external to being, from which it is separate, but as the 'sphere from which the Other, the poor as conditioned by the dominant system, gets justice as a non-part of our world'.[72] Dussel here takes up the perspective of the philosophy of Zubiri, Theunissen and above all Levinas,[73] who has shown how beyond totality there is the Other. But if Levinas's other is individuated on the phenomenological level (all Western philosophy could be said to be phenomenological by definition), the Other of the philosophy of liberation is grasped in his alienation, in his being oppressed and dominated, and with a view to a project of liberation: 'Philosophies can be very humanistic (within the dominating totality), but both the philosophy of Aristotle and that of Hegel justify the *status quo* of their social formation.'[74]

The Other, external to the system, is thematized in three variations which form the three sections of a philosophy of liberation: politics, eroticism and pedagogy. Politics has as its theme the externality of the dominated people on the international scale and the exploited people on a national scale; eroticism has as its theme the relationship beween the domination of the male over the female and analyses male ideology and praxis (this is also the sphere in which feminist theology moves); and finally pedagogy takes up and develops the intuitions of the Brazilian pedagogue Paulo Freire and the philosopher of culture Ivan Illich, adopting the theme of the cultural externality of the 'despised cultures' and the 'marginalized races' and putting forward a pedagogy of the oppressed and a new system of popular education.[75] The movement of a philosophy of liberation is not just dialectical; it does not remain internal to the system, but comes close to the reality external to the system, to the reality of the other, with a movement which Dussel defines as analectical (*ana* = beyond), which therefore goes beyond the reality explored by dialectic.[76] Liberation is thus presented as a de-totalizing category, going beyond systems, and the philosophy of liberation as a 'post-modern, popular, feminist philosophy, a philosophy of youth, of the oppressed, of the condemned of the earth, of the condemned of the world and of history'.[77]

IBID.. 9
F. MORENO Rejón
"Teología moral des de los pobres"

3 · The Liberation Theology Controversy

The International Theological Commission's *Dossier* on the theology of liberation

At the end of 1974 the International Theological Commission had decided to study the phenomenon of liberation theology by setting up a sub-committee presided over by Karl Lehmann. Four extensive reports were presented in the plenary session of 2-9 October 1976, in which the theology of liberation was examined from various angles: methodological and hermeneutical (Karl Lehmann), biblical (Heinz Schürmann), ecclesiological (Olegario González de Cardedal) and systematic (Hans Urs von Balthasar). A declaration was extracted from the four reports of the sub-commission and the discussion which followed in plenary session which was approved by the International Theological Commission and published at the end of the four reports in the form of a theological *Dossier* on the theology of liberation (1977). If the four reports go into the merits of the theology of liberation from different points of view, the declaration is not limited to the theme of the theology of liberation but deals more generally with 'Human Promotion and Christian Salvation', a theme which lies at the centre of that theology.[1]

The *Dossier* of studies by the International Theological Commission recognizes the theology of liberation as prophecy from the Latin American church: 'This prophetic cry of Latin American Christianity, confronted with the great poverty and the infinite misery of its society, is the real nucleus of the theology of liberation.'[2] 'The theology of liberation has a specific position in a theo-

42

logy of the kingdom of God, and calls for practical action on the part of the church in shaping the world in accordance with Christ',[3] but at the same time the *Dossier* points out and stresses the unilateralism and the ambiguity of the complex 'theological movement'. The concluding declaration of the International Theological Commission *Dossier*[4] focusses attention on identifying and developing the correct relationship that must be instituted between the *salvation* which comes from God and the *human promotion* which is the work of man: if human advancement is recognized as the 'constitutive element of the Christian proclamation', in the sense that it is an 'integral part' of it, it is necessary to avoid both a monistic identification and a dualistic separation of the two entities, but rather to institute a correct dialectical relationship which affirms simultaneously both the 'unity of connection' and the 'difference'. In the face of the tendencies of contemporary theology, with evident reference to the theology of liberation, the International Theological Commission recalls that the differences between Christian salvation and human promotion come together at a deeper level – maintaining the unity of the connection.

Although some critics[5] have noted that the *Dossier* of the International Theological Commission inclines towards the dualistic position, the argumentative tone of the studies and the Declaration remain flexible, in that there is an explicit awareness of the 'varieties and flexibilities of the phenomenon of the theology (or theologies) of liberation', and engages in dialogue, in that it is open to further investigations, in recognition of the difficulty of making the topic specific in the various social contexts; 'This unity of connection, like the difference which indicates the relationship between human promotion and Christian salvation, should be the specific object of research and new analyses; without doubt this is one of the main tasks of theology today.'[6]

The Vatican *Instruction on Certain Aspects of the Theology of Liberation*

The *Instruction on Certain Aspects of the Theology of Liberation* which was produced by the Congregation for the Doctrine of the Faith on 6 August 1983 and was officially published on 3 September 1984 does not make any reference to the *Dossier* of the International Theological Commission. The main objection that the Vatican *Instruction* makes to the theology of liberation, from which all the others derive, is that it uncritically adopts Marxist analysis within theological discourse: the adoption of this analysis leads to an acceptance of the whole ideology of Marxism and that in turn results in a perversion of Christian faith (VII.6). The ideological nucleus of Marxism which is accepted functions *a priori*, as a hermeneutical principle determining theological discourse (VIII.1), resulting in the radical politicization of the affirmations of faith and theological judgments (VIII.6) which is exemplified above all in ecclesiology (the theory of the church of the people as a class church, IX.11-12) and in christology (an exclusively political interpretation of the christological truths of the tradition, X.9-12).

The Vatican *Instruction* is concerned throughout to clarify some important points which deserve to be stressed: (*a*) in the Introduction it recognizes the incompleteness of its approach, which it plans to take further and complete in a further document, which 'will detail in a positive fashion the great richness' of the theme of Christian freedom and liberation, from both a doctrinal and a practical perspective; (*b*) it recognizes that the aspiration of the people for liberation is one of the principal signs of the times that the church is called to examine in the light of the gospel (I.1); (*c*) it is aware of the complexity of the phenomenon of the theology of liberation which tries to give articulate expression to this aspiration and which is described as a 'theological and pastoral movement' (III.2) in which a plurality of currents can be identified, so that it is in order to speak of 'theologies of liberation' (VI.8); (*d*) it therefore does not mean to mix them all up indiscriminately but to concentrate critical attention on ideological positions (VI.,8-9); (*e*) it authoritatively forbids the ideological use of the document by those who are contributing towards maintaining the wretchedness of the peoples (XI.1); in the last paragraphs the *Instruction* sums up and commends the theme of the theology of liberation to the universal church: 'The Church, guided by the Gospel of mercy and by the love for mankind, hears the cry for justice and intends to respond to it with all her might. Thus a great call goes out to all the Church' (XI.1-2).

In what now goes under the name of the 'Boff case', the topic in dispute was not, at least not directly, the theology of liberation, but some ecclesiological theses put forward by the Brazilian theologian in the volume which has already been quoted: *Church: Charism and Power* (1981). In them he presents the hypothesis of a transition from a hierarchical ecclesiology to a pneumatological ecclesiology, which he claims is already coming to birth in the practice of the grass-roots communities of Latin America. The ecclesiological principle of Boff's book could be summed up as being the primacy of the charismatic principle over the hierarchical principle. In connection with this formulation Roman theology recalls two principles, put by Cardinal Ratzinger like this: (*a*) the constitution of the church is hierarchical by divine institution; (*b*) in the church there is a hierarchical ministry essentially bound up with the sacrament of order. At all events there remains the problem of how best to integrate the experience of the basic communities into ecclesiological theory and the practice of the church and how best to balance the hierarchical element with the charismatic element in the church.[7]

Whereas in the Boff case the point of controversy is well identified, in that the reference is to a specific theological work and a specific author, the terminology of the *Instruction* seems vague, despite the precisions which have been introduced.[8] The following observations could be made with reference to the typology of the theologies of liberation which has already been noted:

Current 1, theology beginning from the pastoral praxis of the church, and current 2, theology beginning from the praxis of the peoples of Latin America, are not touched by the criticism of the document.

Current 4, theology beginning from the praxis of revolutionary Christian groups, is certainly criticized for its generally uncritical acceptance of Marxist analysis. However, it should be noted that qualified observers regard this current as being largely a minority and marginal one, and one that is represented more by popularizers than by authentic theologians.[9]

It remains a matter of controversy whether and to what degree current 3, theology which begins from historical praxis, by far the most significant current, by virtue of its theological vigour and its relevance for the church, is censured. From these theologians the *Instruction* calls for at least work on clarifying some positions and some aspects of their theological reflection which can prove ambiguous and lead to misunderstanding.

Where are the problems? In substance, two charges are made against the theology of liberation: first, that it takes over the Marxist analysis of society, thus running the risk of turning Christian faith into an ideology; second, that it favours the formation of a parallel church, the *Iglesia popular*, in opposition to the official church represented by the bishops. These are the two main points which the current process is meant to clarify.

(*a*) On the theme of Marxism Gutiérrez says more precisely: 'Certainly the social sciences are used in the study of social reality, but not that which is known as "Marxist analysis", certainly not – as Fr Arrupe put it - "exclusively".'[10] The Boff brothers also deny that Marx is either the father or the godfather of liberation theology. 'All in all Marxism was always used as a *mediation* in the service of something greater, which is faith and its historical demands. It is used to clarify and to enrich some significant theological notions: people, poor, history, and also praxis and politics. All in all it is an operation of *Aufhebung*: acceptance and critical transcendence.'[11] It seems that the *Instruction* understands Marxism as a rigid doctrinal system and as a precise political system, while the theologians of liberation usually have a select and differentiated relationship to the analyses which sociological schools with a Marxist orientation make of the structures of exploitation.[12] In that case, where elements are taken over from Marxist analysis they are used to show in a more convincing way how such an acceptance is a critical one and how

46

the elements taken up can be integrated into the specific horizon of Christian theology.

Connected with the theme of Marxism is that of *violence*. On the basis of the situation in Latin America a distinction is usually made between three types of violence: the first is the violence which is institutionalized in the very structures of the dominant social order; the second is the repressive violence used to defend this first violence; the third is counter-violence. The theology of liberation has never developed a 'theology of violence' (or better, of counter-violence), a reflection which has been carried on for some time in Europe within the theology of revolution but which even in this context has proved problematical.[13] Moreover, the theology of liberation does not have its own particular reflections or its own particular solution to the theme of violence: 'Theological reflection on violence, or in this case more specifically on counter-violence, has not made substantial progress since Thomas Aquinas',[14] and in general takes up what was said at Medellín, which quotes *Populorum progressio* (n.31): 'Although it is true that revolutionary insurrection can be legitimate in the case "of an evident and prolonged tyranny which seriously infringes the basic rights of the person and harms the common good of the country in a dangerous way", if it comes from a manifestly unjust person or structure, it is also certain that violence or "armed revolution" is generally "the source of new injustices, introduces new imbalances and causes new disasters"' (*Peace*, 18). So it should not be difficult for the theology of liberation, which has its infrastructure in peaceful church basic communities operating in a 'terribly peaceful' continent (Juan Luis Segundo) as compared with the history of the European continent, to endorse these principles as a guideline for its reflection and action.

(*b*) In addition to Marxism (and the associated theme of violence) a second source of difficulty for the theology of liberation is the concept of the *Iglesia popular*. The theologians of liberation have explained that this is not a strictly theological concept, but a sociological one; it does not denote an alternative church opposed to the institutional church but the attempt of the church to go down into the masses of the people and into popular culture. Puebla firmly advised against using this term and European theologians who are open to what is going on in church and theology in Latin America advise against stressing this description, given the ambiguity of the term.[15] It will be the task of the theology of liberation to bring together these indications and develop a more correct link between the preferred option for the poor, the catholicity of the church and the universality of Christian love.

The rooting of the theology of liberation in the church, demonstrated by the remarkable fact that the theologian Leonardo Boff was accompanied to the colloquium in Rome by authoritative Latin American bishops and further evidenced by its very structure, in that it does not practise academic or solitary theology but a theological reflection on a communal basis, seems to be a guarantee that the controversy will be the occasion for the necessary clarifications within the Christian communities in Latin America.[16]

If on the basis of the Vatican document it is possible to speak of the 'light and shade of the theology of liberation',[17] it is also possible to turn the expression upside down and speak of the 'light and shade of the Vatican text on the theology of liberation'.[18] Cardinal Aloysius Lorscheider described the less positive aspects of the *Instruction*, in the perspective of the pastoral responsibility of the Latin American church and as a contribution to the development of the second document which was promised:[19] (*a*) It says nothing about the spiritual roots of the theology of liberation, which make it an ecclesial reality: 'The *Instruction* omits a basic question which is at the root of all the theological force of the theology of liberation. What is this basic question? The theology of liberation arises out of a spiritual experience... The theology of liberation cannot be reduced to an immanentist project for transforming social and historical reality... Starting from here the theology of liberation is profoundly ecclesial.' (*b*)

The purely theoretical perspective in which the *Instruction* moves is different from the dynamic nature of the theology of liberation, which does not begin from a theme but from a liberating practice; in other words, the Roman document does not see the peculiarity of the theology of liberation as a second act: 'The approach to the theme of liberation made in the *Instruction* is different from that made in the theology of liberation. The approach in the *Instruction* is from the theme itself... Now the perspective of the theologians of liberation in Latin America and the Third World is different. For them liberation is not a theoretical theme... The theologian of liberation begins from a praxis, from a practice, from the practices of the oppressed... It is a matter of developing a theology from a praxis of liberation. This presupposes an organic involvement in a specific movement, in a basic community, in a centre for the defence of human rights, in a syndicate.' (*c*) As a result the evaluations of capitalism and Marxism become unbalanced: 'In the *Instruction* there is no true balance between the two antagonists who afflict the world today, capitalism and Marxism... The *Instruction* does not brand the other antagonist, capitalism, which finds its justification in the doctrine or ideology of national security, with the same emphasis.' (*d*) The identification that the *Instruction* makes between the option for the poor and the option for the young seems strange: the first is prophetic, the second is only circumstantial: 'Reading the Puebla document one notes that the prophetic option, preferential and in solidarity for the poor, appears something like 646 times. Considering that the Puebla document has 1310 numbered paragraphs, it is evident even from the statistics that this option had a central position at Puebla.' (*e*) The Roman document is based on an approach which in a word is liberal, according to which society is seen as 'an association or a collection of individuals', which is not capable of grasping 'the strictly structural character of human life'. (*f*) The real danger lies not so much in the assumption of elements of Marxist analysis as in the violent class struggle as a way to the solution of the problems of poverty and oppression: 'In an official document of such importance as that of the Sacred Congregation for the Doctrine of Faith, there would have been an opportunity to avoid the term Marxist analysis, keeping to what the Instruction really wanted to stress and show as prejudicial or dangerous for the Christian faith. If the *Instruction* had been limited to the principle of violent class struggle, bringing out the falsity of the principle of violence as a way to the solution of the problems of justice in the modern world, without referring to Marxist analysis, it would have achieved its aim better.'

Another line of interpretation is not so much interested in indicating silences and less positive aspects, or even distortions and caricatures[20] of the theology of liberation which could be found in the Vatican document, as in investigating the underlying theology of the *Instruction*, which makes it incompatible with the way of doing theology which is peculiar to the theology of liberation. This is the approach taken by Juan Luis Segundo in his learned and detailed *Reply to Cardinal Ratzinger*.[21]

For the Uruguayan theologian the most instructive part of the *Instruction* is the first part (the first six chapters) which gives an explicit evaluation of the theology of liberation, because it is in the first part that that theology develops – the theology which governs the argumentation of the *Instruction* – which in the second part leads to the censuring of the theology of liberation. When in VI.9 the *Instruction* says in the future tense: 'The present document will...', which marks the passage from the first, introductory, part to the second, argumentative, part, according to Juan Luis Segundo: 'The theology of liberation has already been condemned and, even more, the theological reasons for this condemnation have already been exposed.'[22]

Segundo makes a careful inventory of the theology which guides the logic of the document: it tends emphatically – in an oscillatory movement which can be noted in the first six chapters, so that the uneven chapters (1,3,5) express the positive aspects of liberation and reflection on the theme and the even chapters (2,4,6) set the negative aspects over against it point by point – to separate and oppose (and not just to distinguish) the religious dimension from the secular dimension of human history: it is a 'very precise theology in which the religious and the secular are opposed to the point of seeming to exclude a revelation of God whose glory is, according to Irenaeus, the living man, the human man, or if one prefers, the humanized man'.[23] The theology of liberation, however, in its responsible talk about liberation, tends to unite – continuing the logic of the theology of the Council, which has overcome the opposition between transcendence and immanence, between religious and secular, between history and conversion – that which the theology of the *Instruction* tends to separate and oppose. So if the document is read by such a theology, it has a very precise logic of its own, but 'it has not yet demonstrated that in its basic outlines and principles, which are universally known, the theology of liberation is a "grave deviation from the Christian faith", not to mention being "a practical negation of it"'.[24] As for the second part, the author of the *Reply* regards it as being somewhat discontinuous, at any rate less consistent than the first part; he finds it unilateral in its 'annoyance' or anti-Marxist pathos, but all in all values it positively for the useful way in which it points out risks and dangers to which the theology of liberation is certainly exposed.

In substance, the analysis of Juan Luis Segundo accuses the theology of the *Instruction* of being a retrograde step not only in relation to the theology of liberation but also in relation to the theology of the Council. Thus the Roman *Instruction* represents a 'warning' directed at the whole church; what is accused is not only the theology of liberation but the change which took place at the Council and the theological reflection which followed it. 'If the analysis I have made is correct, despite their differences the two parts unite in a point which affects the whole church: the negative evaluation of Vatican II and the post-conciliar period.'[25] With this reading the *Instruction* on the theology of liberation is put in the context of a wider process in which what is at issue is the outcome of a hermeneutical battle over the significance of the theology of the Second Vatican Council.[26]

The Vatican document has also been widely discussed and commented on in Europe and North America. Two lines of interpretation can be identified. One series of theological comments is mainly directed at the text of the *Instruction* and evaluates the theology of liberation from the *Instruction*. These comments expose themselves to the risk (as with the comments at the time of the 1950 Encyclical of Pius XII, *Humani generis*, which evaluated the new theology only on the basis of the papal encyclical, without taking account of the complexity and the newness of the theological movement in question),[27] of over-emphasizing a doctrinal text which explicitly deals only with 'some aspects' of a broad and complex 'theological and pastoral movement'. However, another series of theological comments follows a more committed approach and while simply making appropriate references to the text produced by the Roman Congregation, goes back to the texts of the theology of liberation, on the basis of which, avoiding both canonizations and slashing criticisms, the comments give a differentiated evaluation in the context of the whole problem.[28]

The Vatican *Instruction on Christian Freedom and Liberation*

The 1984 *Instruction on Certain Aspects of the Theology of Liberation* was followed by the *Instruction* of the same Congregation for the Doctrine of Faith on *Christian Freedom and Liberation*, dated 22 March 1986 and published on 5 April,[29] which brings out in a positive way the main theoretical and practical aspects of this theme. 'Between the two documents there exists an organic relationship. They are to be read in the light of each other' (no.2). The second document contains five chapters, divided into 100 short paragraphs, and can be conveniently sub-divided into three parts: the first is a historical introduction (ch.1) and serves to locate the treatment of the theme, which in the second part is predominantly theoretical (chs.2-3), and in the third part is predominantly practical (chs.4-5). If the Vatican Congregation had decided to publish one overall document on the theme, the first document would have made up the final part of the second document – a kind of sixth chapter – in that the particular statements of the first document presuppose the more general statements of the second document.

The first historical part of the *Instruction on Christian Freedom and Liberation* illustrates 'the condition of freedom in the contemporary world'. The modern age, beginning with the Renaissance and going through the Enlightenment and the French revolution, can be described as a process of liberation. This indicates the direction in which the modern process of liberation has moved and the gains which it has made: mastery over nature by means of science and technology, the political and social consequences of the democratic ordering of society, a new awareness of humanity and its freedom acquired by means of the historical and humane sciences. But immediately the dangers and the threats which bear down on humanity because of progress are indicated: in the sphere of dominion over nature, the ecological crisis and the danger of nuclear destruction; in the social and political sphere, individualist ideology, collectivist projects and the new relationships in the international field between the rich countries and the poor countries; in the sphere of the new awareness of humanity, the negative outcome of atheism. Thus there are serious ambiguities about the modern process of liberation: 'Because it has been contaminated by deadly errors about man's condition and his freedom, the deeply-rooted modern liberation movement remains ambiguous. It is laden both with promises of true freedom and threats of deadly forms of bondage' (no.18). From these anxious questions there arises the need to reconsider the problem: 'A new phase in the history of freedom is opening before us' (no.24).

In this analysis the *Instruction* implicitly uses the analyses of the 'limits of growth' (Club of Rome) and the dialectic of progress or Enlightenment (Adorno and Horkheimer) – as indeed the Extraordinary Synod of Bishops also did in 1985 in re-reading the signs of the times.[30] The modern history of freedom is a history which runs into aporia; progress can be turned upside down and become a threat. Here at least two lines of problems are indicated, which it is the task of theology to confront and articulate: the relationship between redemption and emancipation, a theme congenial to European theology, and the relationship between emancipation and oppression, a theme congenial to the theology of liberation.

Emancipation is a key word which sums up the modern history of freedom; redemption is a key word which sums up the nucleus of the Christian message. The modern world pursues liberation by means of self-emancipation; Christianity puts forward and offers liberation by means of redemption. The problem which arises and which confronts the most sensitive European theologian[31] is how to level down the historical contrast between redemption and emancipation, to the degree that the two projects are not seen as alternatives: *either* redemption *or* emanciaption. The task of a responsible theology is not to juxtapose redemption and emancipation (as fundamentalist and integralist movements do), nor at the opposite extreme to sell out redemption in favour of emancipation (which is what a secularized theology, redemption as emancipation, seeks to do), but to correlate critically the Christian offer of redemption with the modern history of freedom and emancipation, which above all is rooted in the Christian heritage. The *Instruction* does not go into the merits of the problem, but the problem is at least indicated.[32]

Moreover the *Instruction* mentions (nos.16-17) new inequalities which have come about in international relationships and movements of emancipation in the young nations; here there is awareness of the urgent questions that the theology of liberation puts to church practice and theological reflection. Here the problem is not so much the relationship between redemption and emancipation as that between the Western history of emancipation and its failure, which is the reality of the domination and oppression of the poor countries, and therefore the problem of the dissimilarity between the bourgeois Enlightenment process of emancipation and the popular process of liberation.[33]

After this historical setting, which outlines the problems, the second part of the *Instruction* (chs.2-3) illustrates the theoretical and doctrinal aspects of the theme. Freedom is self-determination, and the power to decide for oneself; through it a person is his own cause. But the *Instruction* immediately recalls – and this is one of the central points of Christian anthropology – that human freedom is creaturely freedom, and therefore 'shared' freedom (no.29); so it is limited and weak: it knows the experience of sin which in this context is seen as an abuse of freedom, autarchy and the absolutization of a freedom which is only shared freedom.

Talk about liberation presupposes talk about freedom and is a function of talk about freedom. The sequence could be presented as freedom, liberation, freedom. Liberation is a process, and also a complex of processes: 'it involves all the processes which aim at securing and guaranteeing the conditions needed for the exercise of an authentic human freedom' (no.31). Freedom sets in motion a process which is a process of liberation that in turn is aimed at a fuller realization of freedom. To be effective freedom, freedom must aim at creating conditions for the exercise of freedom. If it is not to be abstract or idealistic, talk about freedom must relate to talk about the conditions – political, social, economic and cultural – which make possible the effective exercising of freedom. Freedom is a gift which imposes a task; the freedom given produces a desire for freedom, a demand for effective freedom, acquired freedom. So in the Christian perspective the dimension of freedom and liberation is twofold, as a process set in motion by freedom: the soteriological dimension (freedom as a gift), and the ethical and social dimensions (freedom as a task, liberation as a process, nos.23, 71). If the *Instruction* offers appropriate indications for rooting talk about liberation in the Christian doctrine of freedom, the theology of liberation has the merit of relating talk about freedom to liberation, in other words of stressing the conditions for the effective exercising of freedom:[34] 'Freedom, which is the most acute point of the spirit, is completely conditioned from all sides in its acquisition and in its exercise. It has been a serious failing to have regarded it as a purely spiritual reality; it only exists in a twofold incarnation; in the individual, where it is subject to the determinisms of the body; and in society, where it only expands by means of and in economic, technological and cultural conditions. So freedom emanates from the integral liberation of man, in such a way that evangelization, realized in the freedom of faith, cannot be separated from the promotion of humanity. This rejects an anthropology of an Augustinian type, according to which the world is only a provisional abode, and the body a weight to reduce, where the construction of the world is not related to the kingdom of God. The comment of St Thomas Aquinas in the thirteenth century did not succeed in reabsorbing this dualism which has infected the behaviour and the mentality of the church up to Vatican II, when a proper depth was given to earthly realities. The theology of liberation is in direct line with this...'[35]

Having established these theoretical points, the third part (Chs.4-5) considers the predominantly practical aspects: the liberating mission of the church (Ch.4) and the social teaching of the church on a Christian praxis of liberation (Ch.5).

The mission of the church also has a twofold destination: evangelization and human promotion (also called promotion of justice in human society). This second aspect does not go beyond its mission, but cannot absorb it completely: 'Hence she [the church] takes great care to maintain clearly and firmly both the unity and the distinction between evangelization and human promotion: unity, because she seeks the good of the whole person; distinction, because these two tasks enter, in different ways, into her mission' (no.64). In the context of the liberating mission of the church there is a connection between 'the preferential option for the poor' (no.68) and the basic communities (no.69), and the theology of liberation (no.70). To make this more precise: the preferential option for the poor – also accepted in the Final Report of the 1985 Synod of Bishops – is also called in the *Instruction* 'preferential love for the poor'; this twofold linguistic expression is not aimed at weakening the option of the Puebla conference (no.1134), but arises from the different destinations of the two church documents: the text of Puebla is a document peculiar to the Latin American church and sets out the pastoral choices; the *Instruction*, however, is a Vatican document addressed to the universal church. The basic communities – which are the ecclesial infrastructure of the theology of liberation – are seen as 'a source of great hope for the church' (no.69), provided that they are well located in the local and universal church. The passage goes on: 'Similarly, a theological reflection developed from a particular experience can constitute a very positive contribution, in as much as it makes possible a highlighting of aspects of the Word of God, the richness of which had not yet been fully grasped' (no.70), provided that such reflection does not become ideology, projecting on to the word of God meanings which are alien to it. It seems clear here that the implicit reference is to the theology of liberation, which is not reflection *on* but reflection *from*, in other words contextualized reflection, even if the specific expression 'theology of liberation' is avoided, as in fact also happened in the documents of Medellín and Puebla.

The final Chapter 5 outlines the social teaching of the church on a Christian praxis of liberation. The social teaching of the church offers as a guide to a Christian praxis of liberation principles of reflection, criteria of judgment and directives for action. Among the principles of reflection should be mentioned the principle of solidarity, which is opposed to all forms of social and political individualism; and the principle of subsidiarity, which is opposed to all forms of collectivism. Among the criteria for evaluating situations, structures and systems there is mention in particular of the primacy of persons over structures and therefore of freedom over its objectivizations, but generally the need to intervene in unjust structures is rejected: 'On the other hand, the recognized priority of freedom and of conversion of heart in no way eliminates the need for unjust structures to be changed' (no.75). It follows from this that the concept of sin can be applied to structures only in a derived and secondary sense. Among the directives for action it should be noted how the struggle for justice cannot be understood as 'the struggle of one class against another in order to eliminate the foe. She [the church] does not proceed from a mistaken acceptance of an alleged law of history' (no.77); the church guards against the 'myth of revolution' and instead recommends the course of 'far-reaching reforms' (no.78); it notes as more practicable the path of passive resistance, simply mentioning the doctrine, which is very ancient – put forward again by *Populorum progressio* (no.31) and taken up by the Medellín conference (*Peace*, no.19) – which sees the way of armed struggle only as an extreme course to put an end to 'an obvious and prolonged tyranny which is gravely damaging the fundamental right of individuals and the common good' (no.79); finally, it recommends a widespread programme of cultural transformation.

To sum up, there are two dimensions of an integral liberation: the soteriological dimension and the ethical and social dimension. If on the one hand 'The salvific dimension of liberation cannot be reduced to the socio-ethical dimension, which is a consequence of it' (no.71), on the other hand 'Liberation in its primary meaning, which is salvific, thus extends into a liberating task, as an ethical requirement. Here is to be found the social doctrine of the Church, which illustrates Christian practice on the level of society' (no.99).

The social teaching of the church expounded in the last chapter of the *Instruction* is not a substitute for the theology of liberation and therefore it does not exclude it, in that the social teaching of the church (also called the 'social doctrine of the church') is not presented as a compact and closed dogmatic system, which only waits to be applied: 'Far from constituting a closed system, it remains constantly open to the new questions which continually arise; it requires the contribution of all charisms, experiences and skills' (no.72). We have already seen how one of the key features of the methodology of the theology of liberation is the acceptance of the mediation of social analysis. The theology of liberation generally accuses the social teaching of the church of being a theologism by which it substitutes theology for socio-analytical mediation, as if theology could pronounce on everything without the mediation of science; or even of 'semantic mix' or 'bilingualism', when the socio-analytical mediation is indeed taken up, but only in an approximative and declamatory way, without a correct articulation.[36] But if the social teaching of the church is seen in its open, perfectible and dynamic character – as it is presented in the *Instruction*, in line with the Apostolic Letter of Paul VI, *Octogesima adveniens* (no.42), and moreover also with the Puebla document (nos.472,473) - the theology of liberation can be linked with the social teaching of the church as a further determination in a context of domination and oppression: 'So, we can see that the theology of liberation has no difficulty in linking itself with an open concept of the social teaching of the churches. Rather, it can be enriched by it, just as in turn it can enrich it.'[37]

One might ask how positive the *Instruction on Christian Freedom and Liberation* is compared with the *Instruction on Certain Aspects of the Theology of Liberation* to which it explicitly refers.[38] The second *Instruction* is positive in the sense that it brings out in a positive way the theoretical and practical aspects of the theme of Christian freedom and liberation, but is not necessarily to be evaluated in positive terms over against the theology of liberation, which is never mentioned, apart from two oblique quotations. The first, an indirect one, is in no.2, where the *Instruction* refers to some aspects of the theology of liberation; the second, which is quite abstract, is in no.98, where in the conclusion, which contains a reflection on Mary's Magnificat, there is the statement: 'Thus a theology of freedom and liberation which faithfully echoes Mary's Magnificat preserved in the church's memory is something needed by the times in which we are living.' The only real allusion to the theology of liberation is – as I have already indicated – in no. 70, which recognizes the legitimacy of a 'theological reflection developed from a particular experience' which from the context proves to be the experience of 'commitment to the complete liberation of man' (no.69), though – with an evident reference to the first *Instruction* – 'this reflection may be truly a reading of the scriptures and not a projection on to the Word of God of a meaning which it does not contain' (no.70). The positive element of the second *Instruction* is its recognition above all of the fact that under the influence of the theological and pastoral movement of the theology of liberation the *Instruction* does not limit itself to classical talk on human freedom but the talk about freedom is extended and prolonged into talk about liberation, i.e. about the effective conditions for the exercising of freedom and the necessary processes – historical, social and cultural – for bringing it about, so that talk about freedom is credible and specific; and in doing this it takes up issues, themes and concepts the systematic articulation of which is the specific topic of the theology of liberation. If the *Instruction on Christian Freedom and Liberation* cannot be interpreted, at least in the direct sense, as being positive *about* the theology of liberation, what it says proves to be positive *for* the theology of liberation[39] – and it is in this direction that the comments of the theologians of liberation go. The controversy is not closed, but the second Roman *Instruction* leaves room for a responsible theology of liberation.[40]

4 · Doing Theology in a Divided World

There is an African proverb which goes: 'The eyes of the frog do not stop the giraffe from drinking water in the pond.' The frog, all eyes, could be a paradigm of European (and North Atlantic) theology – a theology which is predominantly academic, developed in universities and in other cultural centres, above all preoccupied with the epistemological science of theological discourse – which has also been widely exported to the countries of the Third World. The giraffe, all muscle, which, untroubled by the eyes of the frog, drinks at the pool and goes its way, is a paradigm of the incipient theology of the Third World which now, finally, has begun to express itself with authority and creativity.[1] The Latin American theology of liberation understands itself as an 'expression of the theology of the Third World'.[2]

Martin Grabmann's *History of Catholic Theology* – one of the classic texts of the historiography of our century – still devoted only some 'brief notes' to 'theology in Hispanic America'.[3] But with reference to the emerging reality of theology and theologians in the Third World, Marie-Dominique Chenu recently asked: 'Shall we not be seeing a new theology – in the way that Latin theology was new in relation to Eastern theology – and not merely a prolongation of the theology established in the West?'[4]

In 1974 a group of Latin American scholars based in Louvain, under the inspiration of the theology of liberation and the guidance of the Belgian sociologist François Houtart and the Argentinian historian Enrique Dussel, began to study the possibility of creating a tri-continental theological conference which would bring together theologians from Latin America, Africa

61

and Asia. In the 'Theology in the Americas' conference in Detroit in August 1975 – which saw the first real confrontation between Latin American theology of liberation, black theology and feminist theology, all of which in various ways move within the horizon of liberation,[5] the Louvain project became even more specific and the Chilean Sergio Torres was asked to study it and to make appropriate contacts. In this way there came into being the Ecumenical Association of Third World Theologians (EATWOT), which represents the most important forum of debate among the theologians of the Third World. It held its first theological conference at Dar-es-Salaam in August 1976.[6] The aim of the Association is to promote 'the continuing development of the Christian theologies of the Third World as a service to the mission of the church and as a testimony to a new humanity in Christ expressed in the struggle for a just society'.[7]

The Dar-es-Salaam conference attempted a first survey of theological reflection in Africa, Asia and Latin America, and ended with the Dar-es-Salaam Manifesto, which can be considered the official birth certificate of Third World theology. It is a theology 'aware of the impact of political, social, economic, cultural, racial and religious conditions on theology', and therefore aware of the need for a new theological approach to the problems, including that of an epistemological rupture: 'We are ready for a radical epistemological rupture which makes commitment the first theological act, thus introducing critical reflection on the praxis of the reality of the Third World.' This passage does not speak explicitly of the theology of liberation, but it indicates the contours of the commitment presupposed by theological reflection: 'We call for a commitment to the promotion of justice and the prevention of exploitation, of the accumulation of riches in the hands of a minority, racism, sexism and other forms of oppression, discrimination and dehumaniz-ation.' This is a theology which does not feel itself to be neutral, and which is therefore attentive to the relationship between theory and praxis. However, the statement indicates only the different approaches and emphases which emerged from the

62

encounter, corresponding to the differences in context: 'Thus whereas the demand for economic and political liberation was perceived as that of offering a vital basis for theological praxis in certain regions of the Third World, theologians of other regions have seen that the presence of other religions and other cultures, racial discrimination and domination, or particular situations like the presence of Christian minorities in societies which are not Christian, bring out other dimensions of the task of theology which are demanding in other ways.'[8]

After the inaugural conference in Dar es-Salaam, EATWOT arranged a series of three other conferences in the three continents of the Third World: in Africa, at Accra, Ghana, in 1977 on the theme of African theology; in Asia, at Wennappuwa, Colombo, Sri Lanka, in 1979 on Asian theology; and in Latin America at São Paulo (Brazil) in 1980 on the ecclesiology of Christian basic communities. A fifth, final, conference was organized by EATWOT in New Delhi (India) in 1981 to sum up the work achieved in the previous quinquennium of shared work (1976-1981). A sixth conference held at Geneva at the beginning of 1982 attempted a first encounter between the theologians of the Third World and the theologians of the First World.[9]

Liberation theology in Africa

The conference arranged by EATWOT in Accra, Ghana in 1977 – the first country in black Africa to achieve independence, in 1957 – was devoted to identifying the first steps of African theology.[10] The first beginnings of an African theology, or more precisely the demand for an African theology – can be discerned in the collected volume entitled *Des prêtres noirs s'interrogent*, published in 1956, produced by some young black priests who were asking questions about the future of the mission of the church in Africa in the midst of the political process of decolonization.[11] Up to that point – from the first papal bulls on the evangelization of black Africa at the beginning of the colonial enterprise – the dominant factor had been a 'theology of the *salus animarum*', or a 'theology of the conversion of those without faith', according to which the black Africans were simply savages to be converted; this was replaced, from the 1920s, in connection with a new missionary awareness, by a 'theology of the *plantatio Ecclesiae*', which was a step forward in that the former theology presupposed a polemical and individualistic approach: the blacks to be saved were souls *sedentes in tenebris et in umbra mortis*, whereas the latter presupposed a positive and communal approach, even if the *plantatio Ecclesiae* was seen as a transposition of the ecclesiastical institution on to the *tabula rasa* of Africanism; by definition the local African churches turned out to be carbon copies of the Western churches which had sent missionaries. Hence the need for a new approach, which found its first timid expression in the 1956 volume that has already been quoted, and subsequently in numerous studies which set out to outline the programme for a 'theology of adaptation' or a 'theology of toothing stones', in that it expressed the need to find the point at which the Christian message had to be inserted, the parallels in certain beliefs, rites, symbols, actions and institutions of traditional African society which might seem compatible with the data of the Christian faith, thus giving an 'African face' to Christianity.[12]

The 'theology of adaptation' won a decisive victory over the conception of the *tabula rasa* of Africanism, which was the tacit presupposition of both the theology of the *salus animarum* and the theology of the *plantatio ecclesiae*, and represented the primary, and more advanced, form of 'African theology' up to the Second Vatican Council. If the Council did not tackle the problems directly, with the doctrine of the local church and the new relationship of dialogue set up with the world religions it determined a change of perspective (even if there was no direct mention of African religions in the texts of the Council).

Further theological reflection has gone beyond the 'theology of adaptation', which is thought to be extrinsic and concordist, in favour of a 'theology of incarnation' which found expression, even at an official level, in the Declaration of the Bishops of

Africa and Madagascar present at the Roman synod of 1974: '...the bishops of Africa and Madagascar considered as completely outdated a certain theology of adaptation, in favour of a theology of incarnation'.[13] The 'theology of the incarnation' of the Christian message in African society and culture is now a broad and varied front of theological development. Here it is worth mentioning theologians from Zaire: Tharcissu Tshibangu,[14] one of the pioneers of 'African theology'; Mushete Ngindu, who puts forward a 'critical African theology',[15] capable of taking in African cultural and religious experience; and O.Bimwenyi, author of an imposing study[16] which treats the whole question systematically, showing the foundations of an authentic 'black African theological discourse' which is not expressed in the reductionist terms of 'Africanization' or 'indigenization' that can be traced back to the 'theology of adaptation', but which consists in the correlation of two polarities: the polarity of revelation and that of Africanness.

If 'African theology' in terms of the 'theology of incarnation' is focussed on the cultural, ethnographic aspect of theological discourse, though without denying or misunderstanding the socio-economic and socio-political aspects, other African theologians, under the manifest influence of the theology of liberation, stress the social aspect and the character of liberation which African theology, too, must assume. Among these, mention should be made in particular of Jean-Marc Ela, from Cameroun. For him, if the preoccupation with ethnography which is 'typically African' becomes exclusive, it ends up by amounting to 'an immense excuse': 'How can one be interested in the culture of the people without being disturbed by the marginalization of the masses who are now becoming objects of folklore?'; 'In the debate between Africa and the gospel, what is at issue is not only the "Western Christianity" which has been imposed by the missions of previous days; it is the Christianity of a society which is structured in poverty and oppression.' There is a need to pass from a theology of adaptation to a theology of incarnation, but at the same to enquire in depth into the incarnation of Christianity in the perspective of the forgotten of the earth: 'In this perspective, the theology which is needed is that which is committed to respond to the "cry of the African man".'[17] The author of *Le cri de l'homme africain*,[18] which can be considered to be one of the most significant texts of African theology along liberation theological lines – puts forward a 'theology under the tree', a theology, that is, 'which is developed far from libraries and offices, by getting alongside illiterate country people in a brotherly way to search for the meaning of the Word of God in situations in which this word reaches them';[19] it is a theology aimed at overcoming the 'Christian Creole'[20] hitherto spoken in the African church, but also aimed at overcoming the clerical rhetoric about 'indigenization',[21] in order to understand and live out the faith 'in the context of the liberation of the oppressed'.[22] 'It is not sufficient to invest in a Christianity of the scrubland which risks being swept away by the process of urbanization which is transforming African society.'[23] 'At a time when Africans, like other people, are facing the shock of modernism in a form which is indissolubly technological and cultural, is not perhaps the liberation of the oppressed the main condition of any authentic inculturation of the Christian message?'[24] Here the 'theology of incarnation' is not understood predominantly in the sense of inculturation but in that of liberation.

This is the horizon against which 'black theology' moves. Though it arose in the United States among the black minorities, it has also emerged in South Africa against apartheid. It found its first cultural expression in a series of lectures given in 1971 in various theological centres for blacks in South Africa. Some of these lectures were collected the next year in a volume of *Essays on Black Theology*.[25] However, not all the 1971 lectures could be included in the volume because in the meantime some of the lecturers had been imprisoned for subversive activities. The 1972 publication, already prohibitively censored, was banned and withdrawn from circulation. *Essays in Black Theology* was then republished in an edition in London, which also added the essays censored in the South African edition, under the title *Black Theology. The South African Voice*.[26] The programme of the various contributors to the volume is expressed in this statement: 'Black theology is in revolt against the spiritual slavery of the black people and against the loss of its human dignity and its value. It is a theology in search of new symbols by which to affirm black humanity. It is a theology of the oppressed, made by the oppressed, for the liberation of the oppressed.'[27] Among the main representatives of black theology of liberation in South Africa mention should be made of Manas Buthelezi,[28] Desmond Tutu[29] and Allan Boesak, who in *Farewell to Innocence*[30] – one of the most relevant texts from this theological approach in Africa – looks for a connection between black theology and African theology on the one hand, and black theology and liberation theology on the other. For Boesak, black theology signifies a 'farewell to innocence' for the church and white theology; to a pseudo-innocence which had been cultivated hitherto but which can no longer be sustained in the face of oppression and the new awareness of the people. In particular, the ideology of apartheid no longer works. But black theology must be understood as theology of liberation, and as such it must seek a link with other theologies of liberation in Asia and in Latin America, or anywhere in the world. The category of liberation theology includes black theology. Africanness denotes totality of life, and it is in the name of Africanness that black South African theology must open itself to other contexts and areas of liberation and recognize that racism is only one of the possible oppressions which must be engaged in total struggle.[31] Black theology must not lapse from contextualized theology into regional theology, but as liberation theology in a black situation must articulate itself in the broader context of a total theology of liberation.[32]

The ecumenical encounter in Accra took note of this complex theological reality and sought to co-ordinate the different lines of African theology, in particular those which stress the cultural aspects and the social aspects, and to connect them with the whole complex of themes of Third World theology. As the Accra declaration puts it: just as oppression is not only cultural but also is exercised in political and economic structures and in the dominant mass media, so African theology must also be a theology of liberation. And in putting the stress on liberation in connection with African theology, it joins forces with all the other theologies of the Third World.[33]

Liberation theology in Asia

The theological conference arranged by EATWOT at Wennappuwa (Colombo, Sri Lanka) in 1978 attempted a first survey of the varied theological reflection in Asia.[34] For the Singhalese theologian Aloysius Pieris, Christian theology in Asia is characterized by two poles: (a) the pole of Third Worldness, i.e. the situation of oppressive poverty in which people in Asia live; this is the socio-economic context common to the theology of the Third World; and (b) Asianness, i.e. the specifically Asian context of culture and religions which is just the same for Asian theology as it is for African and Latin American theology: 'These are two inseparable realities that in their interpretation constitute what might be designated as the Asian context and which is the matrix of any theology that is truly Asian.'[35] However, some theologians subordinate the character of Third Worldness to that of Asianness and put more stress on the cultural and religious dimension of Asian theology, while others subordinate the character of Asianness to that of Third Worldness, and consequently develop Asian theology more as theology of liberation.

Among the theologians more concerned with the pole of Asianness, which does not exclude, but also postulates, the dimension of liberation, special mention should be made of Kosuke Koyama and Choan-Seng Song. In his *Waterbuffalo Theology*, as the title suggests, Koyama puts forward a theology which is contextualized in the situation of Thailand, where he is writing: 'On my way to the country church, I never fail to see a

herd of waterbuffaloes grazing in the muddy paddy field. This...
reminds me that the people to whom I am to bring the gospel of
Christ spend most of their time with these waterbuffaloes in the
rice field. The waterbuffaloes tell me that I must preach to
these farmers in the simplest sentence-structure and thought-
development. They remind me to discard all abstract ideas, and
to use exclusively objects that are immediately tangible.'[36] This
is a theology 'from below', not exactly in the sense in which this
expression was intended in Germany, where it was coined, but
in the sense of a popular theology which Koyama pursues and
develops in close contact with his people, with its religious
sensitivity, its simplicity and also its poverty. In his *Mount Fuji
and Mount Sinai*, in which he refers to a pilgrimage which he
made to the source of Japanese spirituality, Koyama stresses
the need for a creative dialogue between Asian spirituality
(symbolized by Mount Fuji) and biblical spirituality (represented
by Mount Sinai).[37] In *Third-Eye Theology*,[38] the Taiwan Chinese
theologian C.S.Song puts forward a theology which can look at
Christ with Asian eyes, with the third-eye of the Buddhist
tradition, which is the eye of the heart, that transcends reason
and looks towards mystery. This is not an apolitical theology but
a 'theology of the womb',[39] which accompanies a process of the
gestation of a new world.

However, other theologians subordinate the character of
Asianness in Asian theology to that of Third Worldness. This
line is taken by the Catholic theologian Carlos Abesamis from the
Philippines: 'The main and principal characteristic of a truly
Asian theology is its Third Worldness. To highlight this primacy,
we say: Third Worldness is the substantive, while Asianness is
the adjective.'[40] In his *Planetary Theology*,[41] the Singhalese
Catholic theologian Tissa Balasuriya considers the need for a
global reorientation of theology on the basis of a global agenda of
problems on a planetary scale. Balasuriya follows the distinctive
methodology of the theology of liberation, which begins from a
broad analysis of the situation, to arrive at a second stage, with
a second act, at the articulation of theological reflection. The

world system, in fact the result of the territorial and economic expansion of European peoples towards the rest of the world, is a system of economic and cultural domination, characterized by classism, racism, sexism and 'religionism' – a theme noted particularly by an Asian theology – which is the attitude that claims to have a monopoly of God and expresses this in a superiority complex which ignores dialogue and respect for other religions. Hence the need for a new world order and a process of purification through which Christianity has to pass to cease being 'the religion of the Holy Roman Empire, Western culture, and Euro-American capitalism'.[42] To do theology in Asia a theology of liberation is needed,[43] in that Western theology is too bound up with questions which arose in the West and moreover is an extremely conservative pro-capitalist and pro-Western theology. A planetary theology faces problems on a planetary scale with a view to an integral human liberation.

In South Korea the perspective of *Minjung* theology has emerged in the Protestant sphere.[44] *Minjung* is a Korean word which is produced by the combination of two Chinese characters: *min*, which denotes people, and *jung*, which denotes mass. So *minjung* denotes the mass of people, or simply the masses, or even the people: 'The *minjung* is the permanent reality of history. Kingdom, dynasties and states rise and fall; but *minjung* remains as the concrete reality in history which has the experience of the rise and fall of political powers.'[45] The Korean term *minjung* is related to the Greek term *ochlos* in the Gospel of Mark which, unlike the term *laos*, the term for the people as a national entity, serves to denote the needy and the disadvantaged.[46] So *minjung* theology is a theology of the people in the sense that it is a reflection of the people which wants to become the subject of its history: it does not seek to be either a Korean political theology or a Korean theology of liberation, but moves with an originality of its own both on the horizon of the politial hermeneutic of the gospel, characteristic of European political theology, and on the horizon of liberation. It arises out of the rediscovery that the

Christian message has not only a religious dimension but also a political one, and it is rooted in the historical and cultural experience of the Korean people. There is a very expressive word in Korean literature, *Han*, and this remains one of the most characteristic elements of *minjung* theology, to such a degree that it is also called 'theology of *Han*'.[47] *Han* is the collective sentiment of the oppressed people, charged with all the abuses by which the history of Korea is marked. In his poem 'The history of sound', the poet Kim Chi Ha (a convert to Christianity) wrote: 'This small peninsula is full of the clamour of offended spirits. It is full of the struggle of the *Han* of whom so many were killed by foreign invasions, wars, tyranny, rebellion, malignant diseases and hunger. I hope that my words are the womb which bears these sounds, to transmit the *Han* and to communicate an acute awareness of our historical tragedy.'[48] *Minjung* theology seeks to give expression to the *Han* of the *minjung*, to the just indignation of the oppressed people both in the Communist régime of North Korea and in the technocratic régime of South Korea.

The Catholic theologian Aloysius Pieris[49] is looking for an original synthesis between the two dimensions, the religious-cultural dimension or Asianness, and the social dimension, or Third Worldness. Asia is a 'continent of languages' which express its religious, cultural and socio-political diversity, very different from that of Africa and above all of Latin America: 'The irruption of the Third World is also the irruption of the non-Christian world... Therefore, a theology that does not speak to or speak through this non-Christian peoplehood is an esoteric luxury of a Christian minority. Hence we need a theology of religions that will expand the existing boundaries of orthodoxy as we enter into the liberative streams of other religions and cultures.'[50] If a Christian theology of liberation has been able to mobilize itself in a continent like Latin America, this is not the case in Asia, where the Christian presence after centuries of mission has reached only the minute percentage of 2% in a continent which contains almost half the entire population of the world. Here the

71

only possible way is that of a new theology of religions capable of demonstrating, and in some way of exploding, non-Christian soteriologies like Buddhism, Hinduism and Taoism, the revolutionary content that they contain, i.e. the nucleus of liberation in social or macro-ethical terms that they have potentially as soteriologies. Christian theology in Asia must take on the task of becoming the 'Christian apocalypse of the non-Christian experiences of liberation'.[51] This is not a painless operation for the church: 'it must be humble enough to be baptized in the Jordan of Asian religiosity and bold enough to be baptized on the cross of Asian poverty.'[52]

The Final Declaration of the Wennappuwa Conference noted the two principal pressures on an Asian theology, the cultural and the social, but it forcibly stressed the Third World character which links Asian theology to the theology of the Third World: 'To be authentically Asian, theology must be immersed in our historico-cultural situation and grow out of it.' But: 'In this context, we question the academic preoccupation to work toward the so-called "indigenization" or "inculturation" of theology divorced from participation in the liberational struggle in history. In our countries today, there can be no truly indigenized theology that is not liberational.'[53] It is also interesting to note that at Wennappuwa black North American theology – which had begun its dialogue with Latin American liberation theology in the 1975 Detroit 'Theology in the Americas' conference and which had always been represented in the progress of EATWOT from its first conference at Dar-es-Salaam (1976) – has been definitively recognized as 'Third World theology', even if it operates on the North American continent.[54]

Developments and prospects

The course taken by EATWOT[55] came to a first conclusion in the fifth conference of the association which was held at New Delhi in 1971 on the theme 'The Irruption of the Third World. Challenge to Theology'.[56] This made a first survey of the intense

72

work of meetings and discussions spanning three continents. The Third World is a complex concept which has a geographical component: the south of the planet (Latin America, Africa, Asia); a socio-economic component: the underdeveloped and dominated countries; a political component: the countries which are not aligned to the political systems of the First and Second World; and finally a theological dimension: it is the 'bitter fruit of oppression'.[57] In the Final Declaration of New Delhi, the irruption of the Third World on the world scene is described as 'an irruption of exploited classes, marginalized cultures, and humiliated races. They are bursting from the underside of history into the world long dominated by the West. It is an irruption expressed in revolutionary struggles, political uprisings, and liberation movements. It is an irruption of religious and ethnic groups looking for affirmation of their authentic identity, of women demanding recognition and equality, of youth protesting dominant systems and values. It is an irruption of all those who struggle for full humanity and for their rightful place in history.'[58] The irruption of the Third World on the world scene is a historical event which challenges theology; the theology of the Third World arises out of this event, characterized by a new methodology, an 'epistemological rupture' as the Dar-es-Salaam manifesto already put it – for which theology is rigorously conceived of as a second act – and the consensus at which it has arrived through the whole process set in motion by EATWOT – a pledge of solidarity with the poor and the oppressed. The confrontation has produced two main lines of reflection operating in different ways: a theological line more sensitive to the cultural aspects, and one more sensitive to the social and economic aspects: 'We are convinced that a relevant theology for the Third World should include both the cultural and socio-economic aspects of the people's lives.'[59] Inculturation/contextualization and liberation have produced the two poles of Third World theology, but the discussion has shown that no inculturation or contextualization, no incarnation of the Christian message, is viable in the Third World unless it is united with a pledge of liberation which addresses not only the Christian communities but also the other religious communities.

The first phase of the process of encounter inaugurated by EATWOT began on a new stage with a meeting between the theologians of the Third World and a delegation of theologians from the First World in Geneva at the beginning of 1983, on the theme of 'Doing Theology in a Divided World'.[60] The confrontation brought out some points above all: the contribution of feminist theology as a theology of liberation also developed in the First World; the emergence – under the challenge of Third World theology – of new theological lines in the First World, which the Final Declaration of Geneva summed up like this: 'Feminist theology, theology of resistance, European theology of liberation, theology of conversion, theology of crisis, political theology, and radical evangelical theology are some of the efforts expressing the fresh air of repentance and renewal in the First World';[61] and above all the awareness that the rise of Third World theology represents an epoch-making change in the history of Christianity and its theology.

We have already recalled the words with which Marie-Dominique Chenu hailed the 'new birth' of the theology and theologians of the Third World. It is the emergence of a 'new paradigm',[62] which relates to a new periodization of the history of Christianity. The necessarily ecumenical dimension of Third World theology leads to the hypothesis of a 'new Reformation'. The Singhalese Catholic theologian Tissa Balasuriya, author of *Planetary Theology*, puts it like this. 'Personally, I think that [the theology of liberation] is the most important theological innovation since the Protestant Reformation of the sixteenth century';[63] and the Indian Protestant theologian Russell Chandran comments: 'This global and ecumenical movement of concern for justice, commitment, and solidarity can be interpreted as a "new Reformation".'[64] Carlos Abesamis[65] from the Philippines sees three stages in the history of theology: the Semitic stage, during which the theology of the Bible came into being; the Greek stage, which begins with the patristic period and goes

74

up to contemporary theology, in which it is possible to distinguish between the Greek metaphysical stage, which includes the patristic and scholastic periods, and the Greek-historical stage, which foreshadows modern theology; the beginning of Third World theology would thus represent a new third stage. For O.Bimweni from Zaire,[66] it is possible to identify three sharp changes in the history of the church: the change at the apostolic council in Jerusalem, which inaugurated the church of the Gentiles; the change brought about by the evangelization of the barbarians, after the fall of the Roman empire; and the third change, which coincides with the collapse of the colonial system on which the church had relied for support from the period of the great discoveries of the fifteen and sixteenth centuries onwards.

The German theologian Johann Baptist Metz, beginning from the perspective of being at the end of the modern period, divides this history of the church and its theology as experienced so far into three periods: 'The epoch of Jewish Christianity, relatively short in terms of years but fundamental for the identity of the Church and of theology; then the very long epoch within a single culture, even if one with many different strands, in other words the epoch of Hellenism and European culture and civilization up to our own days; and finally the era of a culturally polycentric genuinely universal Church whose first hints and beginnings showed themselves at Vatican II.'[67] With a reference to contemporary theology Metz further identified the current paradigms in the sphere of Catholic theology: the neo-scholastic paradigm, which remains the far side of the problems posed by the Enlightenment; the idealist-transcendental paradigm, which accepts the challenge of the critical rationality of the modern world; and finally the post-idealist paradigm, which accepts the challenge of the new relationship between theory and praxis and therefore also enters into a critical encounter with Marxism. Both European political theology and the theology of liberation can be reduced to the third paradigm.[68] Metz has formulated the following theses on the theology of liberation: '1. The theology of liberation is a legitimate and necessary project of post-idealist theology...; 2.

The theology of liberation seeks to face the challenge of Marxism without yielding to it... 3. The theology of liberation manifests – at least initially – the tense transition from a Western church with a more or less unitary culture and in this sense culturally monocentric, to a world church rooted in many cultures, and in this sense poly-centric, in which moreover the Western European legacy is not destined to be repressed but to be provoked and challenged anew.'[69]

For Jürgen Moltmann[70] too, theology is involved in a process of transition: (a) transition from a confessional period to an ecumenical period: 'The shift to an ecumenical period dissolves the confessional identity hitherto affirmed and calls for the discovery of a new open identity in relational terms. This is the explanation of how an ecumenical spring could follow a confessional autumn characterized by agnosticism about identity'; (b) the transition from a Eurocentric epoch to a human epoch. This is certainly a painful period for European theology, which is observing the rise of new theological centres in Latin America, in Africa and Asia with the danger that the traditional European centres will ultimately be marginalized. Some react to this situation with what might be called 'withdrawal symptoms': 'They just don't want to listen and go on doing their theology'; 'We are Europeans and want to remain Europeans'. Others have what might be called 'imitation symptoms': 'We need a European theology of liberation or an American theology of *Minjung*'. However, what is needed is neither to become rigid nor to fall apart but to accept relativity in connection with others: 'We are Europeans and think as Europeans, but that does not mean that we should be stuck in a Eurocentric mode. We live in the First World, but that does not mean that our theology must inevitably become an ideological expression of the predominance of this First World'; the transition from a period of mechanistic domination of the world to a period of world ecological community; and this theme is above all one of feminist theology.

These are analyses which come from different directions and which converge in seeing the theology of liberation, in the context of the theologies of the Third World, as the sign of a transition which is at present taking place in the history of Christianity and its theology. By its capacity for inspiration and involvement, liberation theology is proving to be more than 'a theological movement'; it is 'theology in movement'.[71] To sum up, the features which characterize the theology of liberation are the following. (a) The methodological newness of the option that this reflection presupposes and the praxis which accompanies it: the problem that it poses is not in the first instance that of the acceptance of Marxist analyses, but that of the relationship between faith and discipleship, between theory and praxis, between orthodoxy and orthopraxis, between eschatological salvation and historical liberations, between the proclamation of the gospel and the context of poverty and oppression. (b) The ecclesiological newness of liberation theology, which consists in the reflection which accompanies the activity of church communities which live out a commitment to liberation with dedication: the problem in the first instance is not that of a class church, but that of the emergence of a new historical model of being the church, the model of the church of the poor, which renews itself from the people, weaving afresh in solidarity the common web of the church. (c) The planetary and ecumenical magnitude of the new approach: even if the theology of liberation does not exhaust the variety of new theological ideas which are emerging in the Third World – which in Africa go under the name of theology of inculturation, contextualized theology and theology of incarnation, and in Asia under the name of a new theology of religions – all this constitutes the common dimension of Third Worldness in African and Asian theology as well. (d) The challenge which liberation theology represents for European and Western theology: this is a challenge which so far has met with a variety of responses which are still disjointed, ranging from feminist theology as the best elaborated form of liberation theology in the Western world to the beginnings of a theology of conversion and the most recent developments in political theology. All in all, then, liberation theology is destined to make

77

a deep impression on the theology and practice of the church and the ecumene.

Appendix

Two Theological Interviews

Gustavo Gutiérrez: 'We cannot do theology in a dead corner of history'

Clodovis Boff: 'Where is the theology of liberation going?'

'We cannot do theology in a dead corner of history'

A conversation with Gustavo Gutiérrez

Fifteen years ago in 1969, a short work which you wrote was published in Montevideo. It was given the title Hacia una teología de la liberación *(Towards a theology of liberation). But the Montevideo text substantially reproduces the text of a lecture which you gave in the Peruvian city of Chimbote the previous year, in July 1968. Can you reconstruct the atmosphere of that 'first beginning'?*

Those years in Latin America were very rich and full of experiences; true, they were full of uncertainty, but also of ways of providing a solution to the problems which we were experiencing and still experience in Latin America; ways pursued in contact with the most profound riches of the Latin American people; ways which we also took with impatience. Some were very keen to begin all over again; others wanted to recover the cultural and historical values of our people; these were years of deep commitment. The commitment may not have been always very well orientated, but it was certainly deep.

For those of us who had pastoral responsibility, these were years in which we asked ourselves about the presence of the gospel and the church in this upsurge of ideas, experiences and currents and we looked for criteria of discernment. It was in this situation that a meeting of priests and lay people was held in Chimbote to try to understand what we were experiencing in our country. I was asked to give a theological report on a theme which at that time was being discussed a great deal: the theology of development. As I prepared my report I became aware that it was more biblical and more theological to talk of a theology of liberation, rather than a theology of development. This was a theology of liberation as a theology of salvation in the specific historical situations in which the Lord offered the grace of salvation. The theme was somewhat polemical, hostile not so much to the concept of development as to the politics for which it was the cover.

I recall having read with great interest the manuscript of your magnum opus, Theology of Liberation, *at that time still in typescript, which then appeared in the Peruvian edition towards the end of 1971 and in the Italian edition early in 1972 (even before the Spanish edition!). What were you doing in the three years between Chimbote and the* Theology of Liberation?

The Chimbote meeting took place in July 1968 – as I have already recalled – a few weeks before the conference of the Latin American episcopate at Medellín. The next year, in November 1969, I took part in a meeting at Cartigny, near Geneva, organized by Sodepax. On this occasion, too, I was asked for a report on the theme which was at that time in fashion, again the theology of development, but I discussed the theology of liberation, giving quite a long lecture which was published the next year in Bogota. This was a more developed treatment with a better structure, which already included the four parts into which the material in the *Theology of Liberation* was then divided. For me it was an occasion to think over the theme of liberation more thoroughly, associating it with the liveliest currents of contemporary theology, and also to make a deeper study of some biblical themes like that of poverty. This text circulated widely in Latin America.

The third period – after Chimbote and Cartigny – was the real drafting of the book, which I did during 1970-1971 in gaps between my pastoral work. *Theology of Liberation* is essentially a development of the two previous works, above all of the report presented to the Sodepax meeting in Geneva.

81

After your magnum opus *you collected your main theological essays together in* The Power of the Poor in History, *which was published in 1979, after the conference of Latin American bishops at Puebla. This is a work which reflects the course of the theology of liberation in the decade between Medellín and Puebla.*

Yes, *The Power of the Poor in History* is a collection of articles, one of which comes even before *Theology of Liberation*, and these essays are to some degree the expression of my reflections over a decade. In reality the theology of liberation developed with the rich and powerful contribution of theologians and Christians in Latin America and beyond. In Latin America there were important church events: first the 1968 Medellín conference, and then the long and important preparation for the Puebla conference which took place at the beginning of 1979. *The Power of the Poor in History* bears the stamp of these church events, the documents of the two conferences of the Latin American bishops and the reflections that they provoked in Latin America.

At the same time it became evident that, not out of an itch for novelty but for the sake of clarity, it was necessary to come to terms with the most recent contemporary theology, and this lay behind my reflections on the theme of the conversation partners of theology, which is one of the central points of the book. Modern theology is addressed to the non-believer, who has been produced by the social revolutions of the eighteenth century and the intellectual awareness of them expressed in the Enlightenment. However, liberation theology, indeed liberation theologies (because liberation theology is not only a reality in Latin America), is addressed to the poor, the non-person. I think that the question of the audience for theologies is a very important point in the series of reflections contained in *The Power of the Poor in History*; it is not developed with the aim of setting black against white, but rather is an attempt to understand theologies at an important historical stage. Reflection on this point led me to study Bonhoeffer, to reflect on the great questions which the great Christian Dietrich Bonhoeffer tried to answer. My intention was to stress the difference between the perspective of European

82

theology and that of the theology of liberation, not to discredit European theology but to make a contrast between its major historical stages and, in the context of this confrontation, the diversity of perspectives of the two theologies. This is a very important reflection with which I am continuing. However, other liberation theologians developed other themes and other topics, like christology, ecclesiology and sacramental theology; yet others stressed the racial, the cultural or the feminist perspective in liberation theology. These are elements which can also be found in my essays collected in *The Power of the Poor in History*, but other theologians have developed them more fully.

In the September 1981 number of the Peruvian journal Paginas *I read your profound meditation on 'The God of Life' which I then re-read in* Quaderni di teologia, *published by the Pontifical Catholic University of Peru (*El Dios de la vida, *Lima 1982). Even in the report to the theological conference of EATWOT in São Paulo, Brazil, in February-March 1980, you put considerable stress on the importance of reflecting on God in the theology of revelation. Would you like to comment on this theme?*

The God of Life is a small work, a short book: it is the development of a lecture which takes up some of the points in my earlier works that deserved to be discussed at greater length.

In a way the theme of theology is God, indeed he is its only themes; theology is interested in other themes to the degree that they are related to this primary theme. My small book recalls that the primary act of theology is contemplation, prayer and commitment to others, in particular to the poorest. In *The God of Life* silence is said to be the primary act. Only after this silence – the silence of contemplation and praxis – is there talking, *logos*, a word, reflection on God. So the small book is an example of the conception of theology as a second act, which was already expressed in the first pages of *Theology of Liberation*.

A second point of the volume is the recollection that the God of Jesus Christ, the God who is presented throughout the Bible, is the God of life, who gives life and takes it away – as we are told in Deuteronomy (30.15) – confronted with the alternative of life or death. In the Gospel of John Jesus says that he himself is life: he has come to bring life and to bring it in abundance. It was necessary to call attention to this biblical perspective in a continent in which we come up against unjust and premature death.

Here, too, one can note the difference in perspective between European theology and the theology of liberation: European theology is concerned with atheism; the theology of liberation is concerned with idolatry. In the Bible, too, the denial of God is not atheism but idolatry, which is a matter of putting one's trust not in God, but in idols, in Mammon. Mammon is riches as anti-God, which call for the blood of the poor. Worship of Mammon means shedding the blood of the poor in many specific forms assumed by exploitation and oppression in human history. Idolatry is death; the God of Jesus Christ is the God of life. This is a perspective which has also been developed by Jon Sobrino, who speaks of the appearance of the God of life in Jesus Christ. In Latin America we experience the negation of life, and therefore reflection on God for us develops not so much in confrontation with atheism as in this dialectic of life and death.

The theme of God also returns in your book We Drink from Our Own Wells. The Spiritual Journey of a People. *What is the context of these reflections, which take the line of a communal spirituality?*

We Drink from Our Own Wells is the development of a short paragraph on the spirituality of liberation which already appears in the fourth part of *Theology of Liberation*; it is the resumption of a theme which takes into account our experiences in Latin America and re-reads in this perspective some major works of spirituality in our Catholic tradition. It is a plan which I have had since finishing *Theology of Liberation*. And now I have finally succeeded in paying this debt to myself. I have the profound conviction that historically speaking the preferential option for the poor in the process of liberation is the starting point for an encounter with the Lord, for a demanding discipleship and therefore for a spirituality. So it is that this book to some degree completes the discussion begun in *Theology of Liberation*. I took as the title of the book a fine expression from St Bernard of Clairvaux, who rightly stressed experience as the well to drink from in the course of spiritual life. But in Latin America to drink from one's own well means to drink from a bitter cup.

From 1975 on (the first conference in Detroit) liberation theology has been associated with black theology and feminist theology, which also understand themselves to be theologies of liberation; from 1976 (the conference at Dar-es-Salaam in Tanzania) the theology of liberation began a process of association with the other Third World theologies. This is a course which already has a history of its own, but it has also prompted other discussions, critical and hostile. What is the novelty of the theology of liberation and how does it reply to its critics?

If you can talk about novelty, it is twofold: there are two levels. First of all there is the presence of the poor, the irruption of the poor on the Latin American scene and the international scene: the theology of liberation is an expression of this fact. And secondly there is the conviction which has spread about the presence of the church as a sign of the kingdom in the process of liberation: Medellín and Puebla are two great continental expressions of this presence of the church; but there are also others at a national level. If the theology of liberation has brought anything new, it is the commitment of Christians in the process of liberation, the pastoral commitment of the church as a sign of the kingdom. From the beginning, as I have already recalled, I have defined the theology of liberation as a second act; and therefore in theological reflection we depend on a first act. The first act is commitment. As a second act the theology of liberation is aimed at explaining, at accompanying, at helping this commitment on the level of reflection: it is aimed at discerning other pressures, the presence of the gospel in the complexity of the process of liberation. At the level of reflection there is still much to do, but the novelty of our reflection – if there is anything new about it – derives in the last resort from the active and specific

85

presence of the church community in the pressure on the people of Latin America to create a humane and just society which respects the most basic human rights, especially the right to live. The dissemination of the theology of liberation in other areas of the Third World is the expression of a very great and significant fact for the church.

What is one to say about the criticisms? Certainly they are incomprehensible and malicious: people talk of political reductionism, when the theology of liberation has rejected such a position from the very beginning. It should be recalled that Puebla also spoke of a spiritual reductionism, but this did not cause difficulties. We must also take into account mistakes that have been made, expressions which have been used in the theology of liberation which lend themselves to misinterpretation; but in the sphere of the theology of liberation, on the basis of communal affirmations, there are also different stresses. Difficulties also arise from the fact that our reflections have not explored everything: this or that is said to be missing. But from the beginning it has been impossible to make a complete and perfect theology which would cover all the topics of theological reflection.

But the decisive point is this: the theology of liberation tries to take very seriously the complex and at present conflictual situation of Latin America; it cannot avoid the complexity of the situation, which is as it is; and that is where the difficulties begin. But I ask myself: who does not have difficulties in theology? If theology is a second act, it reflects the difficulties of the first act: how difficult it is to understand our Christian presence in Latin America! How difficult it is for our church communities to find their place in the reality of Latin America! These are the difficulties which are reflected at the level of theological reflection. It is a fact that in Latin America we live in a very difficult situation and we cannot do theology as if we lived in a dead corner of history: we have to participate in our history.

The text of your interview was already prepared for publication when the monthly magazine 30 Giorni *published a text by Cardinal Ratzinger on the theology of liberation. What are your first reactions?*

I think that we must take these observations very seriously, since they come from a person who has such great responsibility. They are observations which call for reflection.

A good deal needs to be clarified, so I will limit myself to reaffirming that with reference to the most serious aspects of the theology of liberation its intentions are deeply commensurate with the church and have the aim of contributing to a better presence of the Christian in our reality, in faithfulness to the gospel. In the study of society the theology of liberation certainly makes use of the social sciences, but not of what is known as Marxist analysis, and certainly not, as Fr Arrupe has put it, 'exclusively'. I am well aware of the excesses and ambiguities of some people in this field, but they do not occur in the most significant features of the theology of liberation.

I think that a frank and calm dialogue can make many things clearer. As far as I am concerned the ultimate and most important reason for liberation theology, the preferential option for the poor, is not to be found in social analysis, but in God in whom we believe in the communion of the church.[1]

Where is the theology of liberation going?

A conversation with Clodovis Boff

Clodovis Boff, born in 1944, a Brazilian theologian, brother of the better known Leonardo Boff, is also a liberation theologian. He has written an important work, *Theology and Praxis* (1978, Orbis Books 1987), on the theology of liberation: it was his doctoral thesis presented to and defended at the University of Louvain. It is an enormous study which analyses the epistemological basis of the theology of liberation in the context of a theology of politics: it is not a reconstruction of the lines of liberation theology but only an attempt to make its language more rigorous, constructing an epistemological theory of the theology of liberation. So at an epistemological level his treatment moves on the level of meta-theory. Along with Jon Sobrino's *Christology at the Crossroads*, Clodovis Boff's work is one of the most relevant contributions from those who are now known as the second generation of Latin American liberation theologians.

In your book Theology and Praxis *you bring out well the fact that the theology of liberation is different from European and North Atlantic theology, including political theology, because it uses what you call socio-analytical mediation, taking up the term introduced by Hugo Assmann. In other words, unlike European theology, which gives priority to philosophical mediation, liberation theology makes use of the social sciences, being a theology focussed on praxis. The theology of liberation arises out of the linkage of socio-analytical mediation with hermeneutical mediation. And by adopting socio-analytical mediation the theology of liberation comes up against Marxism. Would you like to say a little more about this very controversial point?*

This is a somewhat theoretical, indeed epistemological problem. In origin it is a real problem: the understanding that the Christian communities want to have of their situation of poverty, suffering and oppression. And when they try to understand their situation in its social context, they use categories which are provided by culture generally. To begin with, these categories are very simple: poverty, underdevelopment, oppression. Here we are not yet at a cultural level: we have not yet met with the social sciences, but only with the reality of oppression felt through the direct experience of the exploitation of the worker or the marginalization of the *barrio*. But then there is a second stage: when this experience and this awareness grow, the communities ask for greater clarification, for an overall vision: they want to see clearly in their situation. And it is at this point that the social sciences come in: they provide words with which they seek to interpret a reality and an experience which is presented as a first act. It is true that the social sciences are very much in their infancy, but they have succeeded in explaining something of social reality.

If theology comes up against the social sciences, it does not do so because the theologians have now discovered the social sciences, or because the theologians have met the sociologists. This is no arbitrary choice. The theology of liberation comes up against the social sciences because the faithful face a specific situation of oppression and marginalization. Liberation theology is an expression of this encounter between faith and poverty. Faith + poverty = liberating faith; theology + sociology = theology of liberation. The organic, indeed umbilical relationship between liberation theology and the communities of liberation should never be forgotten, because it should never be forgotten that the theology of liberation is the theory of a praxis of faith and a community of faith. If the theology of liberation detaches itself from this context, it makes itself absolutely incomprehensible. So the relationship between theology and the social sciences is a relationship demanded by faith and Christian love which seek to be effective.

At this interpretative level Marxism is also present; it displays its credentials as a theory developed from the perspective of the oppressed, and therefore as an explicative theory of their situation. Not many sociological theories have been developed in this perspective. In practice we have on the one hand functionalist theory with Weber, Durkheim, Talcott Parsons; and on the other, Marxist theory. But it needs to be understood that the basic communities see Marxism on the basis of praxis, and for this reason they embark on an instrumental and free relationship with Marxism; they adopt it freely as an instrument of clarification, and for this reason they have a critical and corrective relationship with it. The church communities sense where Marxism does not give an explanation, where it is limited, and they go beyond it, because they have an experiential wisdom, a humanistic wisdom, and above all very great faith which carries them forward. Marx is like a travelling companion who can help to interpret their situation of oppression, but no more than that. This is the point of encounter with Marxism. It is not a cultural debate, from study seminars, which is what happened in Europe during the 1960s. Our problem is the poor and their liberation, and Marxism, too, can help here with its analyses.

On the other hand, if we do not want to take Marxist analysis into account, then there is the problem that capitalism, which is our problem with all its dehumanizing effects, would not be criticized and censured. So to prevent Christian communities and theologians from having such recourse to Marxism is to remain within the capitalist system.

So the novelty of the theology of liberation from an epistemological perspective consists in the adoption of socio-analytical mediation. And this adoption brings with it a reconstruction of hermeneutical mediation, the mediation which is already operative in traditional theological discourse. Would you like to go into more detail about the content of socio-analytical mediation? What is the programme for the communities of liberation? Can it be said that such a historical programme goes 'beyond capitalism and Marxism'?

In the theology that they are developing the basic Christian communities are not seeking to anticipate the future dogmatically; in other words, they are not putting forward very detailed social programmes, because if the social programme has not yet matured it is likely to be illusory and to end up by getting in the way. What can be seen in the experience of the Latin American church and theological reflection is more than a well-defined historical programme; it is a utopia inspired by faith. Such a utopia has two sides: one negative and the other positive.

The negative side is the negation of society as it is, i.e. the negation of an unjust, exploited and inhumane society, But the majority already give a name to such a society and talk of a capitalist society. It can be said that the documents of the Latin American churches are anti-capitalist.

The other side is the positive, or propositive side: the perspective is that of an alternative and new society more in keeping with the ideals of the kingdom. Within this new society a new historical programme can come into being which can also be seen as a third way in comparison with capitalism and Marxism: an enriched historical alternative of the spiritual values of the gospel. This is not a third way in the sense of a new Christianity, but an adoption of the values of the gospel in their rationale of equality, love of the least, brotherhood, solidarity, power as service, a shared economy. It can be said that the gospel is confronted with an unprecedented historical challenge: that of inspiring the development of a more humane historical programme, beyond capitalism and Marxism.

This aspiration has been felt in the course of history: it is now an aspiration at a planetary level which is also making itself felt at the level of international organizations and institutions. And the church, Christians, has a decisive contribution to make to the purification and the historical realization of this approach. We are certainly not alone; we are working with other historical, political and social forces, inspired by other ideologies, but we

91

must make our own contribution towards overcoming a crisis which is not just a crisis in social terms but a crisis of civilization, which involves both the capitalist and the Communist systems.

On 3 September 1985 the Congregation for the Doctrine of Faith published the Instruction on Certain Aspects of the Theology of Liberation; *some days later, on 7 September, your brother Leonardo Boff entered the Palace of the Holy Office to explain the ecclesiological theses put forward in his book* Church: Charism and Power. *Could you explain the connection between these two events?*

The theme of Leonardo's book, which has been the object of examination by the Congregation for the Doctrine of Faith, is an ecclesiological one. The controversial book puts in question the global structure of the church, and therefore also puts in question the hierarchy in that they have the task of co-ordination and communion. Now this ecclesiological theme must be seen as the internal aspect of the theology of liberation. A church of liberation must also be liberated within: a church which seeks to fight for a juster society, for a society in which there is a sharing in the economy, in culture and in power, must have within it a structure of communion and participation in which the voice of the least is heard and where responsibility is shared; this is a structural homology.

The 'conversation' between Cardinal Ratzinger and Leonardo Boff turned on ecclesiological, i.e. internal, questions raised by the theology of liberation. It is impossible to conceive of a church of liberation seeking to be structurally adequate to its liberating mission and its new historical tasks which is authoritarian and hierarchical in its internal structure. That means that the theology of liberation which is the vehicle of a programme of social renewal also has a programme for renewing the church: it is trying to elaborate a new model of being the church which is adequate to historical challenges and the demands of the gospel.

The Vatican Instruction *has provoked a flood of comments, but so far the reaction of liberation theologians has been somewhat reserved and cautious, not least because the episode is not yet closed. What is your evaluation as a representative of the theology of liberation?*

The first attitude of theologians of liberation is that of listening: an authoritative body is speaking to the theology of liberation which defines itself in terms of its roots in its church, which along with its communities, its bishops and its theologians, puts itself in an attitude of communion, and therefore of listening, of respect, of self-criticism. And the first message that we receive – in this attitude of listening – is this: the theology of liberation is a legitimate project and a legitimate task.

Another point that the Roman document forcibly stresses is that Marxism is dangerous to Christian faith because of its totalizing and totalitarian thrust: Marxism is all-devouring, it tends to exhaust rational explanation. But we have already indicated how the problem of the adoption of socio-analytical mediation is raised within the discussion of the theology of liberation.

Having said this, I should add that even confronted with an authoritative Vatican document, we must never cease to be theologians. The theologian is never simply the exegete of the *magisterium*: *magisterium* and theology – as the Pope also recalled in his speech on his visit to Germany – are two autonomous and complementary functions in the service of the people of God. The theology of liberation is not simply the speculative reflection of the *magisterium*. Now, as theologians we also have something to say about the document. It seems to us that the document should have been produced on a less narrow, a broader basis of consultation and elaboration. We feel left out: it is a document composed from outside; you might say that it has the fault of extrinsicism, in that it is written outside the places where theology is developed. And this extrinsicism can be felt not only in individual phrases but in its general spirit, which is abstract, doctrinaire and deductive; it is a way of doing theology which is very different from ours; we begin from the reality which is

93

experienced in our communities. For example, for us poverty also means sin in that it is in contradiction to God's plan; it is not just a sociological datum.

A second theological observation can be associated with the first: in the perspective of the Vatican document liberation is only a theme to reflect on. However, this does not get to the real heart of liberation theology, which is an ecclesial process, that of a church which is struggling in the world and seeking to be its leaven. So the document detaches liberation from the church of liberation, from the experience of a liberating faith. For the document the crucial point is Marxism; for the theory of liberation the crucial point is poverty and oppression. The problem of the adoption of even Marxist categories in the analysis of reality must be put within the wider problem of poverty and oppression.

In the history of European theology we are familiar with the phrase post Bultmann locutum *to indicate the new course taken by theology in German after the hegemony exercised by the theology of Rudolf Bultmann. Could you take up the phrase and in our case speak of a* post Ratzinger locutum: *where is the theology of liberation going after this intervention by Cardinal Ratzinger? How do you see the future?*

It is difficult to make forecasts. I would say that while on the one hand this *Instruction* criticizes possible deviations, on the other it encourages the church, and not just the church of Latin America, but the whole church, to fight for the cause of the poor and of justice. I do not think that it disparages the work that is being done in the church basic communities, where the theology of liberation is coming into being; it does not attack the matrix of the theology of liberation. While there are these groups of Christians, priests, religious, bishops and theologians who are struggling with the poor for their liberation there will always be the possibility of reflecting on this process. And such reflection is called liberation theology. The document criticizes some expressions, some forms, but not the sources or the process of liberation as it is experienced in our communities; the document has also already served to universalize this historical challenge, the challenge of the poor. From this perspective, even though that was not its intention, it could be presented, beyond the limitations that I have recalled, as a contribution which relates to the theology of liberation and its cause. Now the problem is posed on a universal level: *post Ratzinger locutum* – to take up the expression – the theologians of the First World, too, cannot ignore it with ostrich-like politics or play games by criticizing details.[2]

Notes

Preface

1. Cf. in particular, for the most recent contributions, 'Sulla teologia della liberazione', in *Rivista del Clero Italiano* 66, 4/1985, 282-95; 'Teologia e Terzo Mondo', in *Il Progetto* 5, 25-26/1985, 120-3; 'Origine e metodo della teologia della liberazione', in *Rassegna di teologia* 26, 4/1985, 303-24; 'Temi e problemi della teologia della liberazione', in *Rassegna di teologia* 27, 1/1986, 34-62.

1. The Origin and Method of Liberation Theology

1. E.Dussel, 'Sobre la historia de la teología en América Latina', in E.R.Maldonado (ed.), *Liberación y Cautiverio. Debates entorno al método de la teología de la liberación*, Mexico 1975, 19-68. Cf. also E.Dussel, 'Hipótesis para una historia de la teología en América Latina (1492-1980)', in P.Richard (ed.), *Materiales para una historia de la teología en América Latina*, DEI, San José, Costa Rica 1981, 401-52, where the periodization is made even more precise. R.Oliveros, *Liberación y Teología. Génesis y crecimiento de una reflexión (1966-1977)*, CEP Lima 1977, is also interesting on periodization.

2. E.Dussel, 'Sobre la historia de la teología en América Latina', in E.R.Maldonado (ed.), *Liberación y cautiverio*, 62.

3. L.Boff, *Teologia do cativiero e da libertação* (1975), 9.

4. R.Alves, 'From Paradise to the Desert. Autobiographical Musings', in R.Gibellini (ed.), *New Frontiers of Theology in Latin America* (1975), Orbis Books 1979 and SCM Press 1980, 291. But in *Tomorrow's Child: Imagination, Creativity and the Rebirth of Culture*, Harper and Row and SCM Press 1972, Alves added: 'If our child cannot be born in this time, we can at least make of our present the moment of conception' (197).

5. G.Gutiérrez, *Hacia una teología de la liberación*, MIEC-JECI (First series, 16), Montevideo 1969.

6. G.Gutiérrez, *Theology of Liberation* (1971), Orbis Books 1973 and SCM Press 1974.

7. H.Assmann, *Theology for a Nomad Church*, Orbis Books 1976; this is a translation of Part One of the work *Teología desde la praxis de la liberación*, Sígueme, Salamanca ²1976.

8. L.Boff, *Jesus Christ Liberator* (1972), Orbis Books, Maryknoll and SPCK 1978.

9. Cf. the collections of texts on liberation theology, especially R.Gibellini (ed.), *New Frontiers of Theology in Latin America*, Orbis Books 1979 and SCM Press 1980; D.W.Ferm, *Third World Liberation Theologies. A Reader*, Orbis Books, Maryknoll 1986.

10. Cf. *The Church in the Present-Day Transformation of Latin America in the Light of the Council*, two vols., Second General Conference of Latin American Bishops, Medellín, Colombia 1968, Official English edition edited by Louis Michael Colonnese, Latin American Division of the United States Catholic conference, Washington DC. For its historical significance and importance for the church cf. P.Richard, 'La conferenza di Medellin: contesto storico della sua nascita, diffusione e interpretazione', in *Lotta e conversione. La Chiesa latino-americana tra il timore e la speranza* (1980), Editrice Tempi di Fraternità, Turin 1981, 55-64.

11. S.Galilea, *La teologia della liberazione dopo Puebla*, Queriniana, Brescia 1979, 22.

12. E.Schillebeeckx, 'Befreiungstheologie. Zwischen Medellín und Puebla', *Orientierung* 46, 1979, 6-10, 17-21.

13. For the relationship between the reception of Vatican II in Latin America and liberation theology, cf. L.Boff, 'Eine kreative Rezeption des II.Vatikanums aus der Sicht der Armen: Die Theologie der Befreiung', in E.Klinger and K.Wittstadt (eds.), *Glaube im Prozess. Christsein nach dem II.Vatikanum (für Karl Rahner)*, Herder, Freiburg, Basel and Vienna 1984, 628-54.

14. Cf. *Puebla and Beyond*, ed.John Eagleson and Philip Scharper, Orbis Books, Maryknoll 1979. This volume contains a history of events leading up to the conference, a conference report and the official English translation of the Final Document of the Puebla conference, from which quotations in the present book are taken. For developments following the conference cf. C.A.Libanio Christo, *Diario di Puebla*, Queriniana, Brescia 1979. For the course that led from Medellín to Puebla cf. E.Dussel, *De Medellín a Puebla. Una década de sangre y esperanza (1968-1979)*, CEE-Edicol, México 1979, and from another perspective, H.Borrat, *La svolta: Chiesa e politica tra Medellín e Puebla*, Citadella Editrice, Assisi 1979.

15. Cf. J.Sobrino, 'Puebla, serena afirmación de Medellín', in *Christus* (Mexico), 520/1, 1979, 49-51.

16. L.A.Gallo, *Evangelizzare i poveri. La proposta del Documento di Puebla*, LAS, Rome 1983, 101.

17. H.Assmann, *Theology for a Nomad Church*, 37f. The quotation between double inverted commas is of a phrase used by one of those involved in the biblical symposium on the theme of 'Exodus and Liberation' held in Buenos Aires in July 1970, cf. ibid., 35.

18. Cf.G.Gutiérrez, *La pastoral de la Iglesia en América Latina*, MIEC-JECI, Montevideo 1968, which includes part of the author's lecture at the

first meeting of Latin American theologians at Petrópolis in January-February 1964.

19. Cf.G.Gutiérrez, *Theology of Liberation*, 13. This is the definition which appears in the Peruvian edition, *Teología de la liberación*, CEP, Lima 1971, 31. There is a variation in the Spanish edition, Sígueme, Salamanca 1972: the theology of liberation is defined as 'critical reflection on historical praxis in the light of the word' (34). The English translation has 'Christian praxis'.

20. G.Gutiérrez, *The Power of the Poor in History*, Orbis Books and SCM Press 1983, 60.

21. G.Gutiérrez, *We Drink from Our Own Wells. The Spiritual Journey of a People*, Orbis Books and SCM Press 1984, 38.

22. L.Boff, 'Eine kreative Rezeption des II.Vatikanums aus der Sicht der Armen: Die Theologie der Befreiung', *Orientierung* 46, 1979, 640.

23. F.Fanon, *The Wretched of the Earth* (1961), Penguin Books 1967, 9, 23.

24. For a bibliography on the socio-economic theory of dependence in Latin America see the book which contains the minutes of the meeting of the Escorial in summer 1972, *Fede e cambiamento sociale in America Latina*, 1973, Citadella, Assisi 1975, 295-8.

25. G.Gutiérrez, *Theology of Liberation*, 27.

26. Cf. *In Search of a Theology of Development*, Papers from a Consultation on Theology and Development held by Sodepax, Cartigny, Switzerland 1969; *Towards a Theology of Development*, Annotated Bibliography compiled by Fr Gerhard Bauer for Sodepax, Cartigny 1970.

27. H.Assmann, *Theology for a Nomad Church*, 30f.

28. Cf. G.Gutiérrez, 'Teologia e scienze sociali', in *Il Regno-Documenti* 19, 1984, 620-8.

29. P.Hünermann, 'Lateinamerikas Staatsklasse und die Armen. Der gesellschaftliche Ort der Befreiungstheologie', *Herder-Korrespondenz* 10, 1984, 476.

30. For the tasks which arise for the church from this new reading of underdevelopment in the countries of the Third World cf. V.Cosmao, *Changer le monde. Une tâche pour l'Église*, Cerf, Paris 1980.

31. P.Freire, *Educação como Pratica da Liberdade*, Paz Tere, Rio de Janeiro 1967.

32. P.Freire, *The Pedagogy of the Oppressed*, Penguin Books 1972.

33. L.Bimbi, in the Preface to the Italian edition of *The Pedagogy of the Oppressed*, Mondadori 1980, 13.

34. Cf. the distinction made by G.Gutiérrez, *Theology of Liberation*, 36f.

35. G.Gutiérrez, *The Power of the Poor in History*, 211.

36. Among the main surveys of the theology of liberation cf. E.Dussel, *Histoire et théologie de la libération. Perspective latino-américaine*, Éditions Ouvrières, Paris 1974; M.Cuminetti, *La teologia della liberazione in America Latina*, Borla, Bologna 1975; R.Oliveros, *Liberación y teología. Génesis y*

crecimiento de una reflexión (1966-1976), CEP, Lima 1977; A.G.Rubio, *Teologia de libertação: politica ou profetismo*, Loyola, São Paulo 1977; R.McAfee Brown, *Theology in a New Key, Responding to Liberation Themes*, Westminster Press, Philadelphia 1978; N.Greinacher, *Die Kirche der Armen. Zur Theologie der Befreiung*, Piper, Munich 1980; J.Ramos Regidor, *Gesù e il risveglio degli oppressi. La sfida della teologia della liberazioni*, Mondadori, Milan 1981; E.Bernardini, *Comunicare la fede nell'America oppressa. Storia e metodo della teologia della liberazione*, Claudiana, Turin 1982; E.Dussel, *Herrschaft und Befreiung. Ansatz, Stationen und Themen einer lateinamerikanischen Theologie der Befreiung*, Exodus, Fribourg CH 1985 (a collection of fourteen articles on history and philosophical theology published in *Concilium* between 1969 and 1984); J.Arduini, *Horizonte de esperança. Teologia da Libertação*, Edições Paulinas, São Paulo 1986.

The most studied theology is that of G.Gutiérrez: for this theologian cf. the vast monograph by M.Manzanera, *Teología, Salvación y Liberación en la obra de Gustavo Gutiérrez. Exposición analítica, situación teórica-prática y valoración crítica*, Universidad de Deusto, Bilbao 1978; for a general introduction to his thought cf. R.McAfee Brown, *Gustavo Gutiérrez*, Makers of Contemporary Theology, John Knox Press, Atlanta 1980. For the influence of Gutiérrez's work cf. the collected volume *Vida y reflexión. Aportes de la teología de la liberación al pensamiento actual*, CEP Lima, 1983. For the cultural and ecclesial context cf A.Riuzzi, *L'oro del Perú: la solidarietà dei poveri*, EMI, Bologna 1984.

37. C.Boff, *Theology and Praxis. Epistemological Foundations* (1978), Orbis Books, Maryknoll 1987.

38. Cf. the article by L.Boff, which makes a good deal of use of the study by Clodovis Boff, in L.Boff-C.Boff, *Salvation and Liberation. In Search of a Balance between Faith and Politics*, Orbis Books, Maryknoll and Dove Books, Australia 1984.

39. Cf. the bibliography on the theme of 'The Poor, the Church and Theology' in *IDOC-International* 1-2, 1980, 85-95. As an example of narrative theology on the way in which theologians live out this option in practice cf. L.Boff and C.Boff, 'Due teologi in cammino con il popolo dell'Amazonia', *Quaderni Asal* 29-30, EMI, Bologna 1982.

40. The first theorizing on socio-analytical mediation is to be found in H.Assmann, *Theology for a Nomad People*, 110-48.

41. C.Boff, *Theology and Praxis*, 11.

42. Ibid., 59.

43. Ibid., 87f.

44. Cf. J.L.Segundo, *The Liberation of Theology* (1975), Orbis Books, Maryknoll 1976.

45. Cf. the analysis of these documents in R.Muñoz, *Nueva conciencia de la Iglesia en América Latina*, Nueva Universidad, Santiago de Chile 1973; Sígueme, Salamanca 1974.

46. C.Boff, 'Teologia e Pratica', *Revista Eclesiástica Brasileira* 36, 1975, (789-810) 798.

47. J.C.Scannone, 'La teologia della liberazione: caratterizzazione, correnti, tappe', in K.Neufeld (ed.), *Problemi e prospettive di teologia dogmatica*, Queriniana, Brescia 1983, 393-424.

48. Cf. L.Gera, *Teología de la liberación*, Servicio de Documentación MIEC/JECI, 10-11, Lima 1973; J.C.Scannone, *Teología de la liberación y praxis popular. Aportes críticos para una teologia de la liberación*, Sigueme, Salamanca 1976.

49. Cf. S.Torres and J.Eagleson (eds.), *Theology in the Americas*, Orbis Books, Maryknoll 1976.

50. Cf. S.Torres and V.Fabella (eds.), *The Emergent Gospel. Theology from the Underside of History (Papers from the Ecumenical Dialogue of Third World Theologians, Dar-es-Salaam, 5-12 August 1976)*, Orbis Books, Maryknoll 1978.

51. L.Boff, 'Eine kreative Rezeption des II.Vatikanums aus der Sicht der Armen: Die Theologie der Befreiung', 651-3. For a survey of the theological activity of EATWOT (Ecumenical Association of Third World Theologians) cf. E.Dussel, 'Theology of the "Periphery" and the "Centre": Encounter or Confrontation?', *Concilium* 171, 1984, 87-97. On this new reality cf. M.-D.Chenu, 'A New Birth: Theologians of the Third World', *Concilium* 144, 1981, 18-26.

52. G.Gutiérrez, 'Prassi di liberazione, teologia e annuncio', in *Concilium* 6, 1974, 87f. (published at a time when *Concilium* was not appearing in English).

53. Cf. R.Alves, *A Theology of Human Hope*, Corpus Books, Washington DC 1969, with a preface by Harvey Cox,

54. Cf. E.Feil and R.Weth (eds.), *Dibattito sulla 'teologia della rivoluzione'* (1969), Queriniana, Brescia 1970, which includes the texts cited. Cf. also the rich material on the theme assembled in M.E.Marty and D.Peerman (eds.), *Theology and Revolution*, New Theology 6, Macmillan, New York 1969; R.Rendtorff and H.E.Tödt, *Theologie der Revolution. Analyse und Materialien*, Suhrkamp, Frankfurt 1969.

55. J.Comblin, *Théologie de la révolution. Théorie*, Éditions Universitaires, Paris 1970; id., *Théologie de la pratique révolutionnaire*, Éditions Universitaires, Paris 1974.

56. Comblin, *Theologie de la pratique révolutionnaire*, 16.

57. L.Boff, 'Eine kreative Rezeption des II.Vatikanums aus der Sicht der Armen: Die Theologie der Befreiung', 632f. The text in double quotation marks comes from L.Boff and H.Assmann. There are many writers who tend to blur the difference between theology of revolution and theology of liberation: cf. J.Ellul, *Les combats de la liberté*, Étique de la liberté, Vol.3, Centurion and Labor et Fides, Paris and Geneva 1984, 173-97.

58. A. le Mone (ed.), *Teologie dal Terzo Mondo: teologia nera e teologia*

101

latino-americana della liberazione (1973), Queriniana, Brescia 1974: the Geneva symposium was dominated by the feeling of 'Incommunication'.

59. Cf. J.Moltmann's open letter to José Míguez Bonino in R.Gibellini (ed.), *Ancora sulla 'teologia politica': il dibattito continua*, Queriniana, Brescia 1975, 202-17. In the same volume cf. also the text by J.B.Metz from the Madrid conference, 'Chieso e popolo ovvero il prezzo dell'ortodossia', ibid., 175-201, which is interesting because of its connection with liberation theology. Moltmann's letter was occasioned by J.M.Bonino, *Doing Theology in a Revolutionary Situation* (1975), Fortress Press and SPCK 1975, which remains the most important work of political theology by a Protestant theologian. The volume edited by J.V.Pixley and J.-P.Bastian, *Praxis cristiana y producción teológica. Materiales del Encuentro de teologías celebrado en la Comunidad teológica de Mexico (8 al 10 octobre 1977)*, Sígueme, Salamanca 1979, is interesting for the debate between Europe and North American theology and the theology of liberation which it contains; so too is G.Gutiérrez and R.Shaull, *Liberation and Change*, John Knox Press, Atlanta 1977.

60. X.Miguélez, *La teología de la liberación y su método. Estudio en Hugo Assmann y Gustavo Gutiérrez*, Herder, Barcelona 1976.

61. For the theme of praxis in the theology of liberation cf. also P.E.Bonavía Rodrigues, *La prassi nella teologia della liberazione*, Quaderni Asal 30, Roma 1977; F.Castillo (and others), *Theologie aus der Praxis des Volkes. Neue Studien zum lateinamerikanischen Christentum und zur Theologie der Befreiung*, Christian Kaiser and Grünewald, Munich and Mainz 1978.

62. Cf. G.Gutiérrez, 'From the Underside of History', Part IV of *The Power of the Poor in History*, 169-234.

63. Ibid., 191.

64. G.Gutiérrez, 'The Limitations of Modern Theology: On a Letter of Dietrich Bonhoeffer' (1979), in ibid., 229.

65. Ibid., 211. For the relationship between theology and modernity cf. also P.Richard, *Le Christianisme a l'épreuve des théologies de la libération*, Preface, Lyons 1978.

66. C.Boff, *Theology and Praxis*, 20-35, 221-32.

2. Themes and Topics of Research in Liberation Theology

1. L.Boff, *O evangelho do Cristo Cósmico*, Vozes, Petrópolis 1970.

2. L.Boff, *Jesus Christ Liberator* (1972), Orbis Books, Maryknoll and SPCK 1978. Cf. also the essay by Boff, 'Christ's Liberation via Oppression: An Attempt at Theological Construction from the Standpoint of Latin America', in *Frontiers of Theology in Latin America*, 100-32.

3. L.Boff, *Jesus Christ Liberator*, 43-6.

4. Ibid., 240.

5. For the theology of the cross in the context of the theology of liberation cf. L.Boff, *Paixão de Cristo, paixão do mondo*, Vozes, Petrópolis 1977.

6. Cf. the excellent summary: L.Boff, 'Jesucristo Libertador: el centro de la fe en la periferia del mundo', in *La fe en la periferia del mundo. El caminar de la Iglesia con los oprimidos*, Editorial Sal Terrae, Santander 1981 (17-47) 44.

7. Cf. the treatment in the straightforward, but tightly-packed book which he wrote with his brother Clodovis: L.Boff and C.Boff, *Salvation and Liberation. In Search of a Balance between Faith and Politics* (1979), Orbis Books, Maryknoll and Dove Books, Australia 1984, from which the quotations are taken.

8. J.Sobrino, *Christology at the Crossroads*, Orbis Books, Maryknoll and SCM Press 1978. Cf. also J.Sobrino, *Jesús en América Latina. Su significado para la fe y la cristologia*, Editorial Sal Terrae, Santander 1982 (a collection of eight christological studies later than *Christology*, of which the first, which has the title 'La verdad sobre Jesucristo', ibid., 15-93, is important for giving the context of his *Christology*). Cf. J.Alfaro, 'Análisis del libro "Jesus en América Latina" de Jon Sobrino', *Estudios Eclesiásticos* 59, 1984, 237-54.

9. J. Sobrino, 'Jesús y el Reino de Dios. Significado y objetivos últimos de su vida y misión', in *Jesús en America Latina*, 152.

10. J.Sobrino, 'Significado del Jesús histórico en la cristologia latino-americana', in *Jesús en América Latina*, 112f.

11. J.Sobrino, *Christology at the Crossroads*, 105.

12. Cf.J.Sobrino, 'La verdad sobre Jesucristo', in *Jesús en América Latina* (n.8), 82-5.

13. J.Sobrino, *Christology at the Crossroads*, 342.

14. Cf. J.Sobrino, 'La aparición del Dios de vida en Jesús de Nazaret', in *Jesús en América* (n.8), 157-206. For the same theme see G.Gutiérrez, *El Dios de la vida*, CEP, Lima 1982; id., *Parlare di Dio a partire dalla sofferenza dell'innocente. Una riflessione sul libro di Giobbe*, Quiriniana, Brescia 1986; and the composite volume, *The Idols of Death and the God of Life. A Theology*, Orbis Books, Maryknoll 1983. Cf. also V.Araya, *El dios de los pobres. El misterio de Dios en la Teología de la Liberación*, DEI, San Jose, Costa Rica 1983.

15. J.Sobrino, *Christology at the Crossroads*, 117.

16. Ibid., 391f.

17. Ibid., 348f.

18. For the christology of liberation see the study by C.Bussmann, *Befreiung durch Jesus? Die Christologie der lateinamerikanischen Befreiungstheologie*, Kösel, Munich 1980; and the anthology of texts edited by J.van Nieuwenhove, *Jésus et la libération en Amerique Latine*, Desclée, Paris 1986. For the christology of liberation in the context of contemporary christologies see R.Gibellini, 'Le nuove cristologie', in the appendix to F.J.Schierse, *Cristologia*, Queriniana, Brescia 1984, 151-71.

19. For the use of 'epistemological suspicion' see J.Sobrino, *Christology*

at the Crossroads, xvf.; id., 'La verdad sobre Jesucristo' and 'Significado del Jesús histórico en la cristología latinoamericana', both in *Jesus en América Latina*, 28-9, 99-102, where the model of demythologization is integrated with the model of demanipulation as a reaction to the abuses of the name of Christ, and also with the model of depacification in the sense that Christ must not leave the reality of oppression in peace.

20. Cf. J.M.Bonino (ed.), *Jesús: Ni vencido ni monarca celestial*, Tierra Nueva, Buenos Aires 1977. Cf. also H.Assmann, 'The Power of Christ in History: Conflicting Christologies and Discernment', in *Frontiers of Theology in Latin America*, ed. R.Gibellini, Orbis Books, Maryknoll 1979 and SCM Press 1980, 133-50. For the image of Christ present in the history of Latin America see also S.Trinidad, 'Cristología – Conquista – Colonización', in *Cristología en América Latina*, Panorama de la teología latinoamericana VI, Sígueme, Salamanca 1984, 204-20.

21. J.Sobrino, *Christology at the Crossroads*, xvi.

22. L.Boff, 'Jesucristo Libertador: el centro de la fe en la periferia del mundo', in *La fe en la periferia del mundo*, 24.

23. R.Muñoz, *Nueva conciencia de la Iglesia en América Latina*, Nueva Universidad, Santiago de Chile 1973; Sígueme, Salamanca 1974. Cf. the brief summary in his article 'The Historical Vocation of the Church', in *Frontiers of Theology in Latin America*, 151-62.

24. Cf.E.Dussel, *Historia de la Iglesia en América Latina. Coloniaje y Liberación (1492-1973)*, Editorial Nova Terra, Barcelona 1972, ³1974, 219ff.

25. Cf. R.Oliveros, *Liberación y teología. Génesis u crecimiento de una reflexion (1966-1977)*, CEP, Lima 1977.

26. Cf. H.Parada, *Crónica del pequeno concilio de Medellín*, ISAL, Santiago de Chile 1973.

27. P.Richard, *Desarrollo de la teología latinoamericana: 1960-1978* (cyclostyled), quoted by E.Bernardini, *Comunicare la fede nell'America oppressa. Storia e metodo della teologia della liberazione*, Claudiana, Turin 1982, 57.

28. L.Boff, 'Eine kreative Rezeption des II.Vatikanums aus der Sicht der Armen: Die Theologie der Befreiung', in E.Klinger and W.Wittstadt (eds.), *Glaube im Prozess. Christsein nach dem II.Vatikanum (für Karl Rahner)*, Herder, Freiburg, Basel and Vienna 1984, 628-54.

29. Cf. the extensive monograph, A.Quiroz Magaña, *Ecclesiologia en la teología de la liberación*, Sígueme, Salamanca 1983.

30. Cf. I.Ellacuría, 'La Iglesia de los pobres, sacramento histórico de liberación', in *Conversión de la Iglesia al Reino de Dios para anunciarlo y realizarlo en la historia*, Editorial Sal Terrae, Santander 1984, 179-216.

31. I.Ellacuría, op.cit., 199.

32. Ibid., 188.

33. H.Assmann, *Theology for a Nomad Church*, Orbis Books, Maryknoll 1976, 182.

34. G.Gutiérrez, 'Theology from the Underside of History', in *The Power of the Poor in History*, Orbis Books, Maryknoll and SCM Press 1983, 211.

35. J.Sobrino, *The True Church and the Poor*, Orbis Books, Maryknoll and SCM Press 1985.

36. J.Sobrino, 'The Church of the Poor: Resurrection of the True Church' (1978), in *The True Church and the Poor*, 93.

37. Cf.I.Ellacuría, 'Los pobres, "lugar teológico" en América Latina', in *Conversión de la Iglesia al Reino de Dios*, 13-78. For the context of the theme in history and systematic theology cf. J. de Santa Ana, *I poveri, sfida alla credibilità della chiesa. Il ruolo dei poveri nella storia della chiesa* (1977), Claudiana, Turin 1977; N.Greinacher and A.Müller (eds.), *The Poor and the Church, Concilium* 104, 1977; D.Mieth and J.Pohier (eds.), *The Dignity of the Despised of the Earth, Concilium* 130, 1979.

38. Cf. I.Ellacuría, 'La Iglesia que nace del pueblo por el Espiritu', in *Conversion de la Iglesia al Reino de Dios*, 65-79.

39. The first systematic discussions of this concept can be found in the collection edited by F.Soto, *Cruz y resurrección. Presencia y anuncio de una Iglesia nueva*, CRT, Mexico 1978, which gathers together the ecclesiological perspectives which were coming to maturity before the Puebla conference.

40. The most important texts for this deeper understanding can be found in the proceedings of the Fourth International Conference of the Ecumenical Association of Third World Theologians at São Paulo, Brazil, in 1980, on the ecclesiology of the theology of liberation with particular reference to the Iglesia popular; cf. S.Torres and J.Eagleson (eds.), *The Challenge of Basic Christian Communities*, Orbis Books, Maryknoll 1981; and the issue of *Concilium* on the theology of the Third World, L.Boff and V.Elizondo (eds.), *La Iglesia Popular: Between Fear and Hope, Concilium* 176, 1984.

41. For this aspect see in particular the essay by E.Dussel, ' "Populus Dei" in Populo Pauperum: From Vatican II to Medellin and Puebla', ibid., 35-46.

42. L.Boff, 'A Theological Examination of the Terms "People of God" and "Popular church"', ibid., (89-97) 96. Cf. also L.Boff, *La fe en la periferia del mundo. El caminar de la Iglesia con los oprimidos*, above all Part II, 119-205.

43. L.Boff, *Ecclesiogenesis*, Orbis Books, Maryknoll and Collins Liturgical 1986.

44. L.Boff, *Church: Charism and Power. Liberation Theology and the Institutional Church*, Crossroad Publishing Company, New York and SCM Press 1985. For the debate on this book cf. L.Boff and C.Palacio, *Igreja: Carisma e Poder – da Polémica ao Debate Teológico*, Vozes, Petrópolis 1982 (with the bibliography mentioned there).

45. L.Boff, op.cit., 159. Cf. also the collection of essays on ecclesiology by C.Boff, *Comunidade eclesial – Comunidade politica. Ensaios de Eclesiologia politica*, Vozes, Petrópolis 1978.

46. G.Gutiérrez, *Theology of Liberation*, Orbis Books, Maryknoll and SCM Press, 6. Cf. also the section on 'A Spirituality of Liberation', ibid., 203-12.

47. Cf. the collection of essays in *Vida y reflexión*. *Aportes de la teología de la liberación al pensamiento actual*, CEP Lima 1983, published as a survey of the ten years since the publication of G.Gutiérrez, *Theology of Liberation*, in 1971.

48. S.Galilea, *Espiritualidad de la liberación*, Ed.ISPLAG, Santiago de Chile 1973, 6.

49. Ibid., 12.

50. Ibid., 19.

51. Ibid., 22.

52. Cf. R.Schutz, *Lutte et Contemplation*, 1974.

53. Cf.J.B.Metz, *Tempo di religiosi? Mistica e politica della sequela* (1977); J.Moltmann, *The Church in the Power of the Spirit*, SCM Press and Harper and Row, San Francisco, 285f.

54. S.Galilea, op.cit., 35-6. Cf. id., *Contemplación y apostolado*, CELAM-IPLA, Bogota 1973.

55. Cf. L.Boff, *La fe en la periferia del mundo. El caminar de la Iglesia con los oprimidos*, Part III devoted to the spirituality of liberation, 207-62.

56. Cf.J.Sobrino, *Liberación con espíritu. Apuntes para una nueva espiritualidad*, Sal Terrae, Santander 1985, in particular Part I, 21-141.

57. Cf. M.Lange and R.Iblacker, *Witness of Hope*, Orbis Books, Maryknoll 1981.

58. Cf. J.Sobrino, *Liberación con espíritu*, 109-25.

59. Cf. J.B.Libânio, *Discernimento Espiritual. Reflexões teológico-espirituais*, Loyola, São Paulo 1977; J.B.Libânio, *Discernimento e Politica*, Vozes, Petrópolis 1977.

60. Cf. G.Gutiérrez, *We Drink from Our Own Wells. The Spiritual Journey of a People*, Orbis Books, Maryknoll and SCM Press 1984.

61. Ibid., 5.

62. Ibid., 19.

63. Ibid., 137. The expression is not just metaphorical, cf. the testimony 'Il grido dal pozzo profondo', in C.Antoine, *America Latina in preghiera* (1981), Citadella, Assisi 1983, 18ff.

64. G.Gutiérrez, op.cit., 136.

65. G.Gutiérrez, 'Reflections from a Latin American Perspective: Finding Our Way to Talk about God', in V.Fabella and S.Torres (eds.), *Irruption of the Third World: Challenge to Theology*, Orbis Books, Maryknoll 1983, 225. The writings of bishops like Oscar Romero, Helder Camara, Antonio Fragoso, Leónidas Proaño, Pedro Casaldáliga, Sergio Méndez Arceo, Evaristo Arns, Aloysius Lorscheider, and writers like Ernesto Cardenal, Carlos Alberto Libanio Christo and Arturo Paolo follow the same line as the spirituality of liberation. Of the biblical scholars who follow this pattern of reflection mention should be made in particular of Carlos Mesters, José Severino Croatto, Porfirio Miranda, George Pixley and Elsa Tamez.

66. Cf. E.Dussel, *A History of the Church in Latin America: From Colonialism to Liberation*, Eerdmans, Grand Rapids 1981. Cf. also the

project of CEHILA (Comisión de Estudios de Historia de la Iglesia en América Latina) for a new *Historia general de la Iglesia en America Latina* in 11 volumes to be published in Spanish and Portuguese-Brazilian. For the epistemological lines of this project cf. E.Dussel, 'Periodizzazione di una storia della chiesa in America Latina', in *Cristianesimo nella storia* 3, 1982, 253-86.

67. E.Dussel, *A History of the Church in Latin America*, 81.
68. Cf. P.Richard (ed.), *Materiales para una historia de la teologia en América Latina*, DEI, San José, Costa Rica 1981.
69. J.S.Scannone (ed.), *América Latina: filosofía y liberación*, Editorial Bonum, Buenos Aires 1974, 3 (this collection also includes a report by A.Salazar Bondy, 'Filosofía de la dominación y filosofía de la liberación', ibid., 5-9).
70. J.C.Scannone, op.cit., 3.
71. E.Dussel, *Filosofía de la liberación*, Universidad Santo Tomas, Bogota 1980, 12.
72. E.Dussel, 'Modern Christianity in Face of the "Other" (From the "Rude" Indian to the "Noble Savage")', *Concilium* 130, 1979, 49-62; the whole issue is dedicated to the theme of *The Dignity of the Despised of the Earth*.
73. Cf. E.Dussel, *Concilium* 96, 1976, who quotes the following works: Xavier Zubiri, *Sobre la esencia* (1963); Michael Theunissen, *Der Andere* (1965); Emmanuel Levinas, *Totalité et Infini*, 1961.
74. E.Dussel, *Filosofía de la liberación*, 91.
75. Cf. the interesting analysis by E.Dussel, *Filosofía de la liberación*, 85-129.
76. Ibid., 212-15.
77. Ibid., 9. The literature on moral theology in the context of the theology of liberation is itself enormous; cf. the summary bibliography by F.Moreno Rejón, *Teología moral desde los pobres. Planteamientos morales de la teología latinoamericana*, PS editorial, Madrid 1986.

3. The Liberation Theology Controversy

1. The texts have been collected together in the volume produced by the International Theological Commission: cf. the Spanish edition edited by K.Lehmann, *Comisión teológica Internacional: Teología de la liberación*, BAC, Madrid 1978.
2. K.Lehmann, 'Problemas metodológicos y hermenéuticos de la "teologia de la liberacion"', in *Teología de la liberación*, 28.
3. H.Urs von Balthasar, 'Reflexiones histórico-salvíficas sobre la teologia de la liberación', in *Teologia de la liberación*, 181.
4. Cf. 'Promoción humana y salvación cristiana. Declaración de la Comisión Teológica Internacional', in the appendix to the volume *Teología de la liberación*, 183-210.

5. Cf. in particular J.I.González Faus, 'La declaración de la Comisión teológica internacional sobre la teologia de la liberación', in *Christus* 43, 1978, 8-22; N.Greinacher, *Die Kirche der Armen. Zur Theologie der Befreiung*, Piper, Munich 1980, 66-70.

6. Cf. the 'Declaración', in *Teología de la liberación*, 203. The English text of the *Instruction on Certain Aspects of Liberation Theology* is published by the Catholic Truth Society, 1984, and quotations are taken from it.

7. Cf. the documentation collected in the volume *Il caso Boff*, EMI, Quaderni EMI/SUD, Sezione ASAL, 1, Bologna 1986.

8. The *Herder-Korrespondenz* dossier 10/1984 on the theme *Befreiungstheologie im Widerstreit*, in particular the article by G.Burchardt, *Rom urteilt zu undefiniert. Etappen eines noch ungelösten Konflikts*, ibid., 480-7, stresses the linguistic ambiguity of the document from the perspective of its vagueness.

9. Cf. the interesting interview with the Vice-chairman of the Peruvian Episcopal Conference, Mgr Dammert: 'La réflexion théologique doit se poursuivre', in *L'actualité religieuse dans le monde* 17, 1984, 9-10.

10. Cf. the dossier published in *Il Regno-Attualità* 8/1984, on the theme *La teologia della liberazione tra accusa e difesa*, (189-96) 192. Gutiérrez refers to the Letter to the Provincials of Latin America sent by Fr Pedro Arrupe on 8 December 1980. The text to which he refers goes: First of all it seems to me that we can welcome, in view of our analysis of society, a certain number of methodological points derived more or less from Marxist analysis, on condition that we do not give them an exclusive character.' Cf. the text of the Letter published in the volume of documents edited by B.Chenu and B.Lauret, *Théologies de la libération. Documents et Débats*, Cerf/Centurion, Paris 1985, (97-104) 98.

11. Cf. the Dossier in *Il Regno-Attualità* 8, 1984, 196.

12. Cf. L.A.Gómez de Souza, 'Breve nota sobre a análise marxista', in *Classes populares e Igreja nos caminhos da história*, Vozes, Petrópolis 1982, 41-54 (the article appeared earlier in *Revista Ecclesiástica Brasiliera* 152 of December 1978 in the number devoted to preparations for the Puebla conference). For the theme cf. R.Fornet-Betancourt, 'Der Marxismusvorwurf gegen die lateinamerikanische Theologie der Befreiung', *Stimmen der Zeit* 4, 1985, 231-40; and the collected volume edited by P.Rottländer, *Theologie der Befreiung und Marxismus*, edition liberación, Münster 1986.

13. Cf. A.Plé (ed.), *À la recherche d'une théologie de la violence*, Cerf, Paris 1968, in particular the essay by P.Blanquart, 'Foi chrétienne et révolution', 159-81: 'When the true revolutionary makes use of violence technically, whether he is a believer or not (i.e. when violence seems to him the appropriate means), he remains in the utopian tension of non-violence: in fact he knows, in terms of human rationality, that he cannot play with fire with impunity, either on his own account or on that of others. He knows that the use of violence also leaves deep traces and long scars in the one who

resorts to it, and that nothing is so harmful to a revolution as useless violence' (p.179).

14. G.Gutiérrez, 'Teologia e scienze sociali', in *Il Regno-Documenti* 19, 1984, (620-8) 628 n.19. The article, originally published in the Lima review *Paginas* (Vol.9, nos.63-64, September 1984, 4-15), is one of the most instructive comments on the theme of the relationship between theology and the social sciences in the context of the theology of liberation. It is included in the volume edited by G.Gutiérrez, *La verdad los hará liberes. Confrontaciones*, CEP, Lima 1986.

15. Cf. E.Schillebeeckx, 'Offices in the Church of the Poor', *Concilium* 176, 1984, 98-107.

16. For documentation cf. *Il Regno-Attualitá* 8/1984; 16/1984; *Il Regno-Documenti* 17/1984; 19/1984; the *Dossier-Adista* 8 on theology of liberation; the proceedings of the National Congress of *Testimonianze* 1, 1985 on the theology of liberation, and above all: B.Chenu and B.Lauret (eds.), *Théologies de la libération. Documents et Débats*, Cerf/Centurion, Paris 1985; N.Greinacher (ed.), *Konflikt um die Theologie der Befreiung. Diskussion und Dokumentation*, Benziger, Zurich, Einsiedeln and Cologne 1985.

17. Cf. the well-documented article by P.Vanzan, 'Luci e ombre della teologia della liberazione', *La Civiltá Cattolica* 1985, II, 342-56.

18. Cf. J. de Santa Ana, 'Luces e sombras no texto vaticano sobre a teologia de libertação', *Revista Eclesiástica Brasiliera* 44, 1984, 176 (completely devoted to the *Comentários à Instrução sobre a teología da libertação*). Cf. also the comments published in *Revista Latinoamericana de Teología* 1, 1984, 2; in *Servir. Teología y Pastoral* 20, 1984, fasc.107; and in *Misión abierta* 1/1985 on the theme *Proceso a la teologia de la liberación?*. Cf. also the survey by J.Kerkhofs, 'La "réception" de l'Instruction de 1984 en Asie et en Afrique', in *Recherches de Science Religieuse* 71, 1/1986, 111-28.

19. Cf.A.Cardinal Lorscheider, 'Observações a respeito de "Instrução sobre alguns aspectos da teologia da libertação"', *Revista Eclesiástica Brasiliera*, 176, 700-8, from which the quotations are taken.

20. Cf. the article by E.Schillebeeckx, published in the Dutch journal *Volkskrant* and reproduced in the *Revista Eclesiástica Brasiliera* 176, 'A Instrução sobre a teologia da liberação se dirige a um interlocutor errado', 764-7: 'A critical incentive from the pastoral *magisterium* would have been most welcome, but no one felt the need for this caricature of the theology of liberation. This distortion is an insult to millions of Christians who suffer all over the continent' (766).

21. J.L.Segundo, *Theology and the Church. A Response to Cardinal Ratzinger and a Warning to the Whole Church*, Geoffrey Chapman 1985.

22. J.L.Segundo, *Theology and the Church*, 36.

23. Ibid., 64f.

24. Ibid., 95.

25. Ibid., 194. This analysis is in part confirmed by the text of the *Rapporto*

sulla fede (Vittorio Messori in conversation with Cardinal Joseph Ratzinger), Paoline, Cinisello Balsamo/Milan 1985, where in the wider context of the anxious analysis after the Council a text by Ratzinger on the theology of liberation is taken over with some modifications. It had already appeared in some newspapers. In the *Rapporto sulla fede* this text by Ratzinger on the theology of liberation is represented on the one hand as 'a text by "a private theologian"' (183), but on the other hand it is then presented as the basis on which the *Instruction* of the Congregation for the Doctrine of the Faith was written (198).

26. The Final Report of the Second Extraordinary Synod of Bishops (9 December 1985) takes over the preferential option for the poor. Cf. W.Kasper, *Il futuro della forza del concilio*, Queriniana, Brescia 1986, 98: 'With this affirmation the report of the Synod picks up, without going into detail on the controversy, one of the most important aims of the theology of liberation and at the same time goes beyond the somewhat unilateral perspective that we find in the *Instruction on Certain Aspects of the Theology of Liberation*, which it is planned to supplement with a second, more positive document.'

27. Cf. what has been said by the historian R.Aubert, 'La teologia cattolica durante la prima metà del XX secolo', in R.V.Gucht and H.Vorgrimler (eds.), *Bilancio della teologia del XX secolo*, Città Nuova, Rome 1972, 2, 65: 'If one attempts to sum up in a brief epilogue the theological movement as it manifested itself in something of a burst of exuberance around 1950, when the encyclical *Humani Generis* represented the beginning of the descending curve which characterized the last years of the pontificate of Pius XII, it could be said that this theological movement, motivated by a twofold preoccupation, that of a return to the sources and of openness to the modern world, stands in the direct line of what must always be the theology of the church.'

28. Essays on this line are collected in the following volumes: R.Marlé, M.Calderon and G.Petitdemange, *Pourquoi la théologie de la liberation?*, Cahiers de l'actualité religieuse dans le monde, Supplement to no.307, Paris 1985; P.Eicher (ed.), *Theologie der Befreiung im Gespräch*, Kösel, Munich 1985; J.B.Metz (ed.), *Die Theologie der Befreiung: Hoffnung oder Gefahr für die Kirche?*, Patmos, Düsseldorf 1986.

29. The English text has been published by the Catholic Truth Society, from which quotations are taken, London 1986.

30. Cf.W.Kasper, *Il futuro dalla forza del concilio*, 47.

31. Cf. L.Scheffczyk (ed.), *Redenzione ed emancipazione*, 1973, Queriniana, Brescia 1975; T.Pröpper, *Erlösungsglaube und Freiheitsgeschichte. Eine Skizze zur Soteriologie*, Kösel, Munich 1985.

32. For this first chapter of the *Instruction* see the comments by N.Klein, 'Welche Freiheitsgeschichte?', *Orientierung* 50, 1986, 88-9.

33. Cf. G.Gutiérrez. *The Power of the Poor in History*, Orbis Books, Maryknoll and SCM Press 1983, above all Part IV, 'From the Underside of

History', 169-234; E.Dussel, *Filosofía de la liberación*, Universidad Santo Tomás, Bogota 1980; G.Gutiérrez, *La verdad los hará liberes*. *Confrontaciones*, CEP, Lima 1986; in particular the relevant analysis of the section on 'The Road of Liberation', 148-202.

34. For the relationship between freedom and liberation generally cf. N.Schiffers, *Liberazione e libertà* (1971), Jaca Books, Milan 1974; E.Pousset, J.Guillet, A.Solignac, P.Agaesse, *Liberté, libération*, Beauchesne, Paris 1978 (in particular the contribution by E.Pousset).

35. M.-D.Chenu, Introduction to the combined French edition of the two Vatican *Instructions* under the title *Liberté chrétienne et Libération*, Cerf, Paris 1986, III-IV.

36. Cf. C.Boff, *Theology and Praxis. Epistemological Foundations*, Orbis Books, Maryknoll 1987, 84-91.

37. C.Boff, 'The Social Teaching of the Church and the Theology of Liberation: Opposing Social Positions?', *Concilium* 150, 1981, (17-22) 20. For a constructive relationship between the social doctrine of the church and the theology of liberation see F.Kampfhaus, 'Die Verantwortung des Glaubens angesicht erfahrener Ungerechtigkeit. Zum Verhältnis von katholischer Soziallehre und Theologie der Befreiung', *Herder-Korrespondenz* 6, 1986, 282-6.

38. Cf. the first comment on the *Instruction* in Herder-Korrespondenz (5/1986, 205f.), indicated even in the title: 'Wie positiv? Die römische Befreiungsinstruktion'.

39. Cf. the comments by L.Boff, G.Gutiérrez, J.Sobrino and I.Ellacuría reported in *Noticias Aliadas*, Actualidad y Análisis sobre América Latina 23, no.16, 1 May 1986, 1-5; C.and L.Boff, 'Carta abierta ao cardenal prefeito da Congregaçáo da Doutrina de Fé', in *Fohla de São Paulo* of 11 May 1986; C.Boff, '15 tesi sulla teologia della liberazione', *Il Regno-Attualità* 12/1986, 293-6.

40. The letter of John-Paul II to the National Conference of Brazilian Bishops dated 9 April 1986, and therefore later than the second Vatican *Instruction*, affirms that to the degree to which it conforms with the teaching of the gospel, the living tradition and the perennial *magisterium* of the church, 'the theology of liberation is not only opportune but useful and necessary'.

4. Doing Theology in a Divided World

1. The African proverb is quoted and interpreted in this sense by the Kenyan Protestant theologian J.Mbiti, 'The Biblical Basis for Present Trends in African Theology', in K.Appiah-Kubi and S.Torres (eds.), *African Theology en Route*, Orbis Books, Maryknoll 1979, 91.

2. Cf. L.Boff, 'Eine kreative Rezeption des II.Vatikanums aus der Sicht der Armen', in E.Klinger and K.Wittstadt (eds.), *Glaube im Prozess*.

111

Christsein nach dem II Vatikanum (für Karl Rahner), Herder, Freiburg, Basel and Vienna 1984, 651-3.

3. Cf. M.Grabmann, *Historia de la teología católica*, Madrid 1940, 350ff.

4. M.-D.Chenu, 'A New Birth: Theologians of the Third World', *Concilium* 144, 1981, (18-23) 18.

5. Cf. the proceedings of the conference: S.Torres and J.Eagleson (eds.), *Theology in the Americas*, Orbis Books, Maryknoll 1976.

6. Cf. S.Torres and V.Fabella (eds.), *The Emergent Gospel. Theology from the Underside of History. Papers from the Ecumenical Dialogue of Third World Theologians, Dar-es-Salaam, 5-12 August 1976*, Orbis Books, Maryknoll 1978.

7. Cf. the Communiqué, in *The Emergent Gospel*, 273.

8. Cf. the Final Statement, in *The Emergent Gospel*, 259-71, from which the quotations are taken.

9. For an overall evaluation cf. E.Dussel, 'Theologies of the "Periphery" and the Centre – Encounter or Confrontation?', *Concilium* 171, 1984, 87-97.

10. Cf.K.Appiah-Kubi and S.Torres (eds.), *African Theology en Route. Papers from the Pan-African Conference of Third World Theologians, 17-23 December, Accra, Ghana*, Orbis Books, Maryknoll 1979.

11. Cf. *Des prêtres noirs s'interrogent*, Collection Rencontres 47, Cerf, Paris 1956.

12. Cf. the book by the Zaire theologian V.Mulago, *Un visage africain du christianisme. L'union vitale bantu face à l'unité vitale ecclésiale*, Présence Africaine, Paris 1965, which remains one of the most representative works of this kind of theology.

13. Cf. 'Promouvoir l'évangelisation dans la corresponsabilité. Déclaration des évêques d'Afrique et de Madagascar presents au quatrième Synode épiscopal mondial', in *La Documentation catholique* 71, no.164, 17 November 1974, 995.

14. Cf. T.Tshibangu, *Le propos d'une théologie africaine*, Presses universitaires du Zaire, Kinshasa 1974.

15. Cf. M.Ngindu, 'The History of Theology in Africa: From Polemics to Critical Irenics', in *African Theology en Route*, 23-65.

16. Cf. O.Bimwenyi-Kweshi, *Discours théologique négro-africain. Problème des fondements*, Présence Africaine, Paris 1981, which is basic for the history of attempts in the direction of an African theology and for the raising of questions.

17. Cf. J.-M.Ela, 'Identité propre d'une théologie africain', in C.Geffré (ed.), *Théologie et choc des cultures, Colloque de l'Institut catholique de Paris*, Cerf, Paris 1984, 23-54, from which the quotations are taken. The African theologian E.M.Metogo, *Théologie Africaine et Ethnophilosophie. Problèmes de methode en théologie africaine*, L'Harmattan, Paris 1985, also writes decisively and polemically along these lines.

18. J.M.Ela, *Le cri de l'homme africain. Questions aux chrétiens et aux églises d'Afrique*, L'Harmattan, Paris 1980.
19. Ibid., 8.
20. Ibid., 13.
21. Ibid., 124, 130, 146: this is a recurrent theme.
22. Ibid., 116.
23. Ibid., 98.
24. J.M.Ela, *Ma foi d'Africain*, Karthala, Paris 1985, 17.
25. Cf. *Essays in Black Theology*, University Christian Movement, Johannesburg 1972.
26. B.Moore (ed.), *Black Theology. The South African Voice*, C.Hurst and Company, London 1973, published in America by John Knox Press, Atlanta 1974, under the title *The Challenge of Black Theology in South Africa*. Cf. also the collection of essays edited by I.J.Mosala and B.Tlagale, *The Unquestionable Right to be Free. Black Theology from South Africa*, Orbis Books, Maryknoll 1986.
27. Cf.*Black Theology. The South African Voice*, ix.
28. Cf.M.Buthelezi, 'Una teologia africana o una teologia nera?', in R.Gibellini (ed.), *Teologia nera*, Queriniana, Brescia 1978, 95-102.
29. Cf. D.Tutu, *Crying in the Wilderness*, Mowbrays 1982, ²1987; also id., 'The Theology of Liberation in Africa', in *African Theology en Route*, 162-8.
30. Cf.A.A.Boesak, *Farewell to Innocence. A Socio-ethical Study on Black Theology and Power*, Orbis Books, Maryknoll 1977.
31. Ibid., 151.
32. Ibid., 144.
33. Cf. the 'Final Communiqué', in K.Appiah-Kubi and S.Torres (eds.), *African Theology en Route*, 189-95. For a general survey of the themes and currents of African theology cf. A.Shorter, *African Christian Theology*, Geoffrey Chapman 1975; J.S.Pobee, *Toward an African Theology*, Abingdon Press, Nashville 1979; K.A.Dickson, *Theology in Africa*, Orbis Books, Maryknoll 1984; G.H.Muzorewa, *The Origins and Development of African Theology*, Orbis Books, Maryknoll 1985.
34. V.Fabella (ed.), *Asia's Struggle for Full Humanity; Towards a Relevant Theology. Papers from the Asian Theological Conference, 7-20 January 1979, Wenappuwa, Sri Lanka*, Orbis Books, Maryknoll 1980.
35. Cf.A.Pieris, 'Towards an Asian Theology of Liberation: Some Religio-Cultural Guidelines', in *Asia's Struggle for Full Humanity*, (74-95) 74f.
36. K.Koyama, *Waterbuffalo Theology*, SCM Press and Orbis Books, Maryknoll 1974, vii-viii.
37. K.Koyama, *Mount Fuji and Mount Sinai: A Critique of Idols*, SCM Press and Orbis Books, Maryknoll 1985.
38. Cf. C.S.Song, *Third-Eye Theology. Theology in Formation in Asian Settings*, Orbis Books, Maryknoll and Lutterworth Press 1979.
39. Cf.C.S.Song, *Theology of the Womb*, Orbis Books, Maryknoll 1986.

40. C.Abesamis, 'Faith and Life Reflections from the Grassroots in the Philippines', in *Asia's Struggle for Full Humanity*, (123-39) 134.

41. Cf. T.Balasuriya, *Planetary Theology*, Orbis Books, Maryknoll and SCM Press 1984.

42. Ibid., 121.

43. Cf. T.Balasuriya, 'Towards the Liberation of Theology in Asia', in *Asia's Struggle for Full Humanity*, 16-27. This is a theme which is also developed by Latin American theology, cf. J.L.Segundo, *The Liberation of Theology*, Orbis Books, Maryknoll 1976.

44. CTC-CCA (Commission on Theological Concerns of the Christian Conference of Asia), *Minjung Theology. People as the Subjects of History*, Orbis Books, Maryknoll 1981, revised ed. 1983. The main contributors are Suh Nam-Dong, Kim Yong-Bock and Ahn Byung-Mu.

45. Kim Yong-Bock, 'Messiah and Minjung: Discerning Messianic Politics over against Political Messianism', in *Minjung Theology*, 183.

46. Cf. Ahn Byung-Mu, 'Jesus and the Minjung in the Gospel of Mark', in *Minjung Theology*, 138-52. Cf. the collection of essays by him, *Draussen vor dem Tor. Kirche und Minjung in Korea*, Vandenhoeck and Ruprecht, Göttingen 1986.

47. Cf. Suh Nam-Dong, 'Towards a Theology of Han', in *Minjung Theology*, 55-69.

48. Quoted in *Minjung Theology*, 26.

49. In addition to the article quoted in n.33 above cf. his contribution to the New Delhi meeting: A.Pieris, 'The Place of Non-Christian Religions and Cultures in the Evolution of Third World Theology', in V.Fabella and S.Torres (eds.), *Irruption of the Third World: Challenge to Theology*, Orbis Books, Maryknoll 1983, 113-39.

50. Ibid., 113f.

51. A.Pieris, in *Asia's Struggle for Full Humanity*, 94.

52. Ibid., 93f.

53. Cf. the Final Statement, in *Asia's Struggle for Full Humanity*, 152-60. For a survey of Asian theology cf. also D.Elwood (ed.), *Asian Christian Theology. Emerging Themes*, Westminster Press, Philadelphia 1980.

54. Cf. J.Cone, 'A Black American Perspective on Asia's Search for Full Humanity', in *Asia's Struggle for Full Humanity*, 176-90. For North American black theology as theology of liberation cf. the basic text by G.Wilmore and J.Cone (eds.), *Black Theology. A Documentary History, 1966-1979*, Orbis Books, Maryknoll 1979; also B.Chenu, *Dieu est noir. Histoire, religion et théologie des Noirs américains*, Centurion, Paris 1977; R.Gibellini (ed.), *Teologia nera*, Queriniana, Brescia 1978; T.Witvliet, *The Way of the Black Messiah*, SCM Press 1986 and Meyer-Stone 1987.

55. I have not taken into account here the proceedings of the fourth congress of EATWOT at São Paulo, Brazil, 1980, because it was mainly focussed on the ecclesiology of the Latin American theology of liberation, and has already been referred to in the previous chapters: cf. S.Torres and

J.Eagleson (eds.), *The Challenge of Basic Christian Communities. Papers from the International Ecumenical Congress of Theology, 20 February to 2 March 1980*, São Paulo, Brazil, Orbis Books, Maryknoll 1981.

56. Cf. V.Fabella and S.Torres (eds.), *Irruption of the Third World: Challenge to Theology, Papers from the Fifth International Conference of the Ecumenical Association of Third World Theologians, 17-29 August 1981, New Delhi*, Orbis Books, Maryknoll 1983.

57. J.R.Chandran, 'A Methodological Approach to Third World Theology', in *Irruption of the Third World*, 83.

58. Cf. Final Statement, ibid., 191-206, here no.26.

59. Ibid., no.44. For the theologies of the Third World cf. also G.H.Anderson and T.F.Stransky (eds.), *Third World Theologies*, Mission Trends no.3, Paulist Press and Eerdmans, New York and Grand Rapids 1976; T.Witvliet, *A Place in the Sun. An Introduction to Liberation Theology in the Third World*, SCM Press and Orbis Books, Maryknoll 1985; D.W.Ferm, *Third World Liberation Theologies. An Introductory Survey*, Orbis Books, Maryknoll 1986, with the accompanying anthology: D.W.Ferm (ed.), *Third World Liberation Theologies. A Reader*, Orbis Books 1986.

60. Cf.V.Fabella and S.Torres (eds), *Doing Theology in a Divided World. Papers from the Sixth International Conference of the Ecumenical Association of Third World Theologians, 5-13 January 1983*, Geneva, Switzerland, Orbis Books, Maryknoll 1985.

61. Cf. the Final Statement, in ibid., 177-93, here no.56. Cf. also the following studies which are the beginning of a new chapter of theology: R.McAfee Brown, *Theology in a New Key. Responding to Liberation Themes*, Westminster Press, Philadelphia 1978; B.Mahan and L.D.Richesin (eds.), *The Challenge of Liberation Theology: A First World Response*, Orbis Books, Maryknoll 1981.

62. The concept of a 'new paradigm' has been introduced into theology from the epistemology of science by Hans Küng, in his study 'Paradigmawechsel in der Theologie. Versuch einer Grundlagenerklärung', in H.Küng and D.Tracy, *Theologie: wohin? Auf dem Weg zu einem neuen Paradigma*, Benziger and Gütersloher Verlagshaus Gerd Mohn, Zurich, Cologne and Gütersloh 1984, 37-53 (contains the proceedings of the international theological symposium held in Tübingen in 1983). For the problems cf. R.Gibellini, 'Un novo paradigma in teologia?', in *Il Regno-Attualità* 14/ 1983, 328-30.

63. T.Balasuriya, in *The Challenge of Basic Christian Communities*, 259.

64. R.Chandran, in *Irruption of The Third World: Challenge to Theology*, 83. The theme of a 'second reformation', which comes from neither Rome nor Wittenberg but from the poor churches of the earth, is also expressed by J.B.Metz, 'Un nuevo modo de hacer teología: tres breves tesis', in *Vida y Reflexión. Aportes de la teología de la liberación al pensamiento teológico actual*, CEP, Lima 1983, 45-56, esp.50.

65. Cf.C.Abesamis, in *The Emergent Gospel*, 117-19.

66. Cf. O.Bimwenyi-Kweshi, *Discours théologique négro-africain*, 59f.

67. J.B.Metz, 'Theology in the Modern Age, and Before its End', *Concilium* 171, 1984, 13-17. Cf. id., 'Standing at the End of the Eurocentric Era of Christianity: A Catholic View', in *Doing Theology in a Divided World*, 85-90.

68. Cf. J.B.Metz, 'Unterwegs zu einer nachidealistischen Theologie', in J.B.Bauer (ed.), *Entwürfe der Theologie*, Styria, Graz 1985, 209-33.

69. J.B.Metz, 'Thesen zum theologischen Ort der Befreiungstheologie', in J.B.Metz (ed.), *Die Theologie der Befreiung: Hoffnung oder Gefahr für die Kirche?*, Patmos, Düsseldorf 1986, 147-57.

70. Cf. J.Moltmann, 'Theologie im Übergang-wohin?', in H.Küng and D.Tracy (eds.), *Theologie – wohin?*, 17-30, from which the quotations are taken.

71. L. and C.Boff, *Come fare teologia della liberazione*, Cittadella, Assisi 1986, 127.

Appendix

1. Edited by Rosino Gibellini, cf. *Il Regno-Attualità* 8, 1984, 189-92.

2. Edited by Rosino Gibellini, cf. *Settimana* 9, 1985, 6f.

116

Index of Names

117

119

Liberation Theology from Orbis . . .

A THEOLOGY OF LIBERATION, *Gustavo Gutiérrez.* Fifteenth-Anniversary Edition, revised and with a new Introduction by the author. The classic work that "must be read, not once but several times, by those interested in doing theology today." *Commonweal*
542-5 Pb   543-3 Cl

ON JOB, *Gustavo Gutiérrez.* "Inquisitive, brilliant, penetrating: this study brings us closer to Job and to ourselves." *Elie Wiesel*
552-2 Pb   577-8 Cl

WE DRINK FROM OUR OWN WELLS, *Gustavo Gutiérrez.* **Foreword by Henri Nouwen.** "Rooted in the reality of oppression . . . this book calls forth a conversion from self-complacency and self-sufficiency to that of solidarity with the poor." *Catholic New Times*
707-X Pb

INTRODUCING LIBERATION THEOLOGY, *Leonardo Boff and Clodovis Boff.* "Readers looking around for a quick but comprehensive and thorough survey of liberation theology cannot do better than study with the Boffs." *Mercy Amba Oduyoye*
550-6 Pb

THEOLOGY AND PRAXIS, *Clodovis Boff.* "A landmark in theology . . . no theologian, in any area, will ever be able to do without it." *From the Foreword by Adolphe Gesché*
416-X Pb

JESUS CHRIST LIBERATOR, *Leonardo Boff.* "An excellent introduction to the basics of contemporary liberation christology and thought." *The Christian Century*
236-1 Pb

AN ASIAN THEOLOGY OF LIBERATION, *Aloysius Pieris, S.J.* The Sri Lankan Jesuit theologian's first book in English, an important contribution to contemporary Christian theology in Asia.
627-8 Pb   626-X Cl

MY FAITH AS AN AFRICAN, *Jean-Marc Ela.* A bold call to re-read the Gospels with the eyes of Africa's teeming poor.
631-6 Pb

THIRD WORLD LIBERATION THEOLOGIES: An Introductory Survey, *Deane William Ferm,* and **THIRD WORLD LIBERATION THEOLOGIES: A Reader,** *Deane William Ferm, Editor.* "The most comprehensive introduction, in any language, to what may well be the most significant theological development in this century."

Publishers Weekly

515-8/516-6 Pb

SPIRITUALITY OF LIBERATION, *Jon Sobrino, S.J.* A book that outlines the "political holiness" demanded by our times.

616-1 Pb   617-0 Cl

CHRISTOLOGY AT THE CROSSROADS, *Jon Sobrino, S.J.* "The most thorough study of Christ's nature based on Latin American liberation theology."   *Time*

076-8 Pb

TOWARD A JEWISH THEOLOGY OF LIBERATION, *Marc Ellis.* "Its message, the cause of liberation, . . . represents hope for the hopeless, and freedom for the oppressed."   *Robert McAfee Brown*

358-9 Pb

GOD OF THE POOR, *Victorio G. Araya.* "A profound meditation on God's choice to accompany and identify with the poor."

John A. Coleman, S.J.

565-4 Pb   566-2 Cl

MINJUNG THEOLOGY, *Commision on Theological Concerns/ Christian Conference on Asia.* " . . . one of the most creative theologies emerging from the political struggles of Third World peoples."

James H. Cone

336-8 Pb

And introducing a new series . . . THEOLOGY AND LIBERATION

TRINITY AND SOCIETY, *Leonardo Boff.* 622-7 Pb   623-5 Cl
ETHICS AND COMMUNITY, *Enrique Dussel.* 618-9 Pb   619-7 Cl
THE HOLY SPIRIT AND LIBERATION, *José Comblin.* 616-1 Pb
617-0 Cl

Order from: Orbis Books, Dept. CO7, Maryknoll, New York 10545
Or call, toll free: 1-800-258-5838